Jesus
to the Astronauts

Translated by Susanne Flatauer

Gerhard R.
Steinhäuser

CORONET BOOKS
Hodder and Stoughton

First published in Great Britain 1974 by
Abelard Schuman Limited

Coronet edition 1976

Printed and bound in Great Britain for
Coronet Books, Hodder and Stoughton,
St. Paul's House, Warwick Lane,
London, EC4P 4AH
By Richard Clay (The Chaucer Press) Ltd,
Bungay Suffolk

ISBN 0 340 19933 4

Contents

Acknowledgments

Illustrations are reproduced by kind permission of the following: Keystone; Vienna Museum of Art History; Austrian National Library; Toni Schneiders; Siemens; USIS; Verlag Kremayr & Scheriau Library; Votava.

The text of the Authorized Version of the Bible is Crown Copyright and the extracts used herein are reproduced by permission.

'And it came to pass, while he blessed them, he was parted from them, and carried up into heaven.'

Luke 24:51, recorded *c.* 100-130 AD.

Many thousands of years ago the gods assembled at Teotihuacan on the Mexican plateau to consider how the sun (which in those days had disappeared from heaven) might be brought back to its former place. None of the gods was willing to tackle the matter.

In the end they chose Teccuciztecatl and Nanahuatzin the Pockmarked for this difficult mission. For four days both gods underwent careful preparations; then, dressed in special iridescent garments, they were taken to Teotxecalli, the furnace of the gods, where a fire had been burning for four days. This they entered and were carried up into heaven where soon afterwards the sun and the moon appeared and shone once again.

Ancient Toltec legend

Introduction

It requires neither special skill nor—since heretics are no longer burnt at the stake—special courage to represent Jesus of Nazareth not as a demigod but as a simple son of man. It requires just as little skill to show the Bible as it really is: a more or less fortuitous conglomeration of early myths of the gods.

However, this book neither aims nor intends to destroy the world conception of Christianity (the Churches themselves see to that much more efficiently) and then to leave the reader to sweep up the pieces. What alone is important and decisive is to trace the way back to the sources, to the men-gods from the cosmos, the only beings who were ever carried up into heaven.

Thus this book proclaims no new doctrine: it merely attempts to point the way to the future. Each one of us must necessarily discover this way for himself.

1 Gates and sepulchres

On the Meseta plateau between Bolivia and Peru—13,000 feet above sea level and only 10 miles from Lake Titicaca, the highest lake in the world—there lies Tiahuanaco, the most mysterious city on Earth. Nobody can accurately say how old it is and by whom it was constructed.

After the conquest of the country by the Spaniards, the Incas replied to questions from the viceroy Toledo and asserted that these structures had always been there. But the ruins of walls and temples (for Tiahuanaco was first and foremost a temple city), jointlessly joined from gigantic blocks of stone, are silent.

At a congress in Paris in 1911 Professor Posnansky, one of the most eminent authorities on the history of ancient America, estimated the age of Tiahuanaco to be 13,000 years, and earned the scorn and hostility of his learned colleagues.[1] Figures suggested by other scholars vary between 1000 and 6000 years; however, according to astronomical calculations based on calendar stones and other relics, the American Rudolph Muller has recently arrived at an estimated figure of 9300 to 14,600 years.

Some time ago, the ethnologist Wendell Bennett[2] made an interesting find: in one of the city's well-shafts he discovered two stone sculptures, one of which was 9 feet high and the other more than 23 feet. Both depicted bearded men with rather European features. According to Indian legends, these are supposed to be effigies of earlier gods who were the founders of Tiahuanaco.

3

But the strangest and most enigmatic monument in Tiahuanaco is the famous 'sun gate'. This is a solid block of stone, a monolith about 9 feet high and 12 feet wide and weighing about 10 tons. Into the stone an oblong opening—a gate about 6 feet high and 32 inches wide—has been hewn (perhaps 'cut' would be a better word). The lintel is covered with several rows of square figures, in the centre of which is enthroned a god also carved out of the stone, with a sun-shaped circle around his head: hence the name 'sun gate'.

As with most of the other buildings, the stone from which this monolith is fashioned was quarried on the other side of Lake Titicaca. How these 'Super-Lego' building blocks, often weighing dozens or even hundreds of tons, got from the quarries to Tiahuanaco remains a mystery, even assuming that at one time the city was situated by the shore of the lake.[3] Stone wheels and cylinders found by Wendell Bennett and Verill—and disproving incidentally the legend that the original inhabitants of South America did not have the wheel—might suggest an explanation, but is it the right one? What remains unanswered above all is the purpose of the sun gate.

It stands in a square of the temple area measuring 142 by 147 yards, completely isolated and not adjoining any other building. There can be no doubt that it never served as either entrance or exit of any building. Could it have been some kind of triumphal arch—perhaps the first in the world?

However, this does not seem very likely, for priests and believers alike would have had to squeeze through the relatively narrow opening one by one, and it must be assumed that those exceedingly skilled stonemasons could easily have made the gate both wider and higher for so important a purpose.

It would seem, therefore, that they wanted it precisely this way and no other. Why?

Up to now very few have investigated these questions, although possibly they hold the key to Tiahuanaco's greatest secret.

For the time being, and from our digression to the Meseta, we may profitably note the following facts:

In the distant past, according to legend and pictorial tradition, gods from the Universe—whether they were called Huiracocha, Huitzilopochtli or whatever, is irrelevant—are said to have landed in this area, where they created a new race of men by whom they were later worshipped in the temples of Tiahuanaco and elsewhere.

In Tiahuanaco there stands the sun gate, an object with no recognizable purpose or meaning, whose function as a gate seems to be almost a matter of secondary importance, and where the things that go with it—its important side parts and powerful super-structure—dominate.

At all events the sun gate is many thousands of years old. The exact figure does not matter as far as we are concerned. It is at least as old as, and probably older than, the temple buildings of Luxor and Karnak in Egypt, from which it is separated by several half--continents and one entire ocean, and which, despite Thor Heyerdahl's raft journeys, we can scarcely take to have been designed and built by the same architect.

Yet similar characteristics can be seen even here: doors or gates are narrow and in glaring disproportion to their compact and clumsy side parts. This would be logical and understandable in a castle or fortress: strong gate towers guard a narrow (and thus readily defensible) entrance. But in a temple? There one might surely expect gates of great and inviting splendour, as was the case later in the sacred buildings of Islam and Christianity.

Not so, however! Apparently the architects of ancient Egypt (certainly no less able than their Persian-Islamic and mediaeval-European colleagues) kept to the same strange 'prescription' as the builders of the sun gate of Tiahuanaco.

Could it be that they had in mind the words of the Gospel according to St Matthew, recorded two thousand years later? 'Enter ye in at the strait gate ... Because strait *is* the gate, and narrow *is* the way, which leadeth unto life ...' (Matt. 7:13-14)

Tiahuanaco ... Egypt ... St Matthew's Gospel ... the 'strait

5

gate' which leads 'unto life': These could be parallels, connections, links. We shall trace and investigate them, from their beginnings to the present time, and to a logical and reasonable explanation.

But first another, similar, chain of apparently inexplicable connections will have to be produced.

This chain stretches from the Pacific to Golgotha.

On the south coast of New Guinea lives the tribe of the Kiwai. They have a national hero, just as the Germans had Siegfried and the Swiss William Tell.[4]

He is, or rather was, called Sido and seems to have been some kind of demigod. It is worth noting, by the way, that his name—although he belongs to a Papuan tribe in the South Seas—contains the same 'sid-' stem as the Latin word *sidus* ('star, constellation, heavenly body').

And Sido does indeed have a connection with the stars. As the Kiwai relate, he had some task to carry out in the sky long ago. In order to get there Sido lay down in a pit, from where he was carried up to heaven in a radiant light after a few days.

The parallel with the Toltec gods Teccuciztecatl and Nanahuatzin here is obvious: demigods or gods enter a 'pit'—Teotxecalli, the furnace of the gods—and subsequently ascend to the stars, somehow transformed.

We encounter the pit or sepulchre again as an aid towards a complete bodily resurrection on the other side of the globe (and that several centuries *before* the birth and death of Jesus of Nazareth), in Babylon.

In those days they held ritual 'festivals' in honour of the god Bel-Marduk.[5,6] During these ceremonies, which occurred at regular intervals, Marduk—represented, according to custom, by a chosen sacrificial 'stand-in'—was arrested, sentenced, whipped and then executed together with a criminal, while a second criminal was set free. A woman then washed the body of the dead god which had been pierced by a lance; it was then taken to a 'mountain' and placed in a rock grave. Three or four days later, Bel-Marduk—presumably in the person of a second (and in this role more fortunate) stand-in—returned alive.

If reports about this little-known cult are correct—and there can be no grounds for doubting them—there is not really much scope left for the authors of the later Jesus myth to come up with a different 'version'.

However, what we are concerned with at this point is simply the factual statement that all over the world traditions and customs regarding the death and resurrection of divine beings had the same sequence: a more or less voluntary walk into a 'furnace' or 'sepulchre', and resurrection (and ascension into heaven) after three or four days. From Mexico through New Guinea and Babylon to Jerusalem: in this context, Christ is only *one* of the later executants of a precisely laid down ritual. Side by side with him, claiming equal status in tradition, are the fates of other gods and demigods: of Dionysius of Thrace (called Eleuthereus = redeemer!); of the Syrian god Adonis; of the god Sandan of Tarsus (native city of the apostle Paul); and of the Sumerian-Akkadian god Tammuz, a 'shepherd god'; and far to the north, where the Germanic god Odin, wounded by a lance, [sic] hung in a tree for three nights and three days before he awoke once more.

Be they Nanahuatzin, Sido, Bel-Marduk, Christ or Odin—everywhere the sequence is the same, and so are the 'props'.

Even if it were possible to assert that at all times and in all places men had had similar ideas of the gods they fashioned, endowing them with similar qualities, such as that of resurrection, there still remains one vital criterion:

> After his earthly death, any 'invented' god would have either risen immediately or after one, two or five days: and yet, at all times and in all places, we find that portentous period of three to four days. This cannot be fortuitous any more than the preceding ceremonies which, apparently, were most intricate.

There is more to this than meets the eye: these rituals represent some earlier reality, subsequently handed down by men in a more or less distorted fashion, even when they no longer knew anything about that reality.

There must have been real models, real gods and real ascensions.

The existence of 'neighbours in the Universe' was regarded as 'most probable' by the American Academy of Science in June 1972 (see page 27), and yet with a similar degree of likelihood it may be assumed that foreign intelligences from outer space—whose technological knowledge was far in advance of that of the Earth dwellers—have visited our planet on more than one occasion.

No matter why these gods came and what they did here, they appear to have come to our planet and left it again by some means. Up to now it has been assumed (from Robert Charroux through Erich von Däniken to Karl F. Kohlenberg) that they did so in spaceships; there are in fact a large number of references to such phenomena in tradition, myth and legend.

But that does not in the least rule out the possibility of their having used hitherto unrecognized means, such as perhaps some form of 'transport' outside of time and space from one point in the Universe to another, with the help of the mysterious 'gates'.

How might we envisage such a form of transport?

Every schoolboy today knows the principle and structure of a high-voltage pilot plant. Between control desks and power units there are large discharge columns at relatively short intervals; when the plant is switched on, powerful flashes of lightning flicker back and forth between them: electrical energy, the energy of our world.

Let us now assume—hypothetically to begin with—that these gods of long ago possessed still other forms of energy, or forces, which not only psychologists but also physicists have lately begun to investigate. We refer to what is known as psi, the force that acts in clairvoyance, thought-transference, telekinesis and other phenomena, and which, according to research by Americans and Russians,[7,8] appears to be at least partly independent of time and space, belonging to another plane or dimension.

That there are more than the four dimensions known to us—length, breadth, height (=space) and time—has been accepted as a matter of course by mathematicians ever since Gauss, Riemann and Lobatchevski. A 'leap' through a fifth dimension, for instance, might carry us—theoretically for the time being—across almost any distance in space without a time-lapse. As a result of recent intensive research into the powers of psi, this is no longer a figment of the imagination. Admittedly, psi energy is known to us only through tests and experiments with men and animals: it can be neither measured nor produced by technological means.

It may be assumed, though, that sooner or later this will become possible. After all, at one time, atomic power was completely unknown and nothing but an empty formula, until in this century it became a very brutal reality.

Moreover, it may be assumed with some justification, and according to the laws of analogy of all technical/physical processes and practices, that plants for the production of 'higher' energy would greatly resemble those we use today for the production of high-voltage electricity. There would be similar control and power units and, likewise, a comparatively narrow discharge field in which (mostly invisible because not belonging to our world and dimension) artificially produced psi energy would be effective. In these fields and gates the space—time framework would be, so to speak, torn asunder, while an opening into and through other dimensions was formed.

What would happen to a man or an object going, or being taken, through such a gate? Well, at that very moment we should be under the impression that the man had disappeared, while at exactly the same moment he would reappear somewhere else, where there was an appropriate reception plant, a counter-gate; for in between there would be no space at all.

Science fiction is wrong in asserting that during such a transport both men and objects would first be broken down (as in television and radio technology) into waves or vibrations and then put together again. That would be neither necessary nor possible

9

And what would those left behind see? An empty opening, perhaps, with a few fluttering discharge waves at the edges, a gate into nothingness, a mirror without a background. Whoever passes through such a gate is suddenly gone without a trace, without smoke, fire or other manifestations—a circumstance, incidentally, which has cost hundreds and thousands of mankind's most valuable members their lives. (I shall explain this statement in detail later.)

Things seem to have happened more effectively during the course of another 'method of ascension' of the gods—the one which later was also ascribed to Jesus of Nazareth. It is based on the principle of partial physical transformation and presumably served other purposes than did transformation effected with the help of the energy gates.

The technical means for this transformation were the 'pits', the 'furnaces' or 'sepulchres'; a better term for these installations might be 'reaction chambers'.

As already mentioned, a resurrection carried out with the help of this kind of installation was bodily visible:

'And it came to pass, while he blessed them, he was parted from them, and carried up into heaven'. Thus Luke reports of Jesus (24:51).

There is a similar report a few thousand years earlier about Quetzalcoatl, bringer of culture to the Toltecs. When his mission had been completed he is said to have set out on his return journey into space from the shore of Yucatán, accompanied by his twin brother Xolotl.[9] He too first made his farewells; he did not then climb into some spaceship, but was carried bodily 'up into heaven'. This, incidentally, was also reported of Hercules by the Greeks: having completed his many heroic deeds on Earth, so the story goes, he climbed onto a 'pyre' on Mount Oite before the eyes of his friends and from there, 'transformed like a serpent which has sloughed its skin', he returned to his father Zeus.

It would therefore seem that the gods had at their disposal at least three means of overcoming time and space, and of ascension: the method known to us again today of travel in spaceships; ascension after a process of physical transformation; zero-time transport through energy gates.

This last possibility was the least comprehensible for the people of that time, and, for that reason, was never described in great detail. But the stone monuments speak of it clearly enough.

On what occasions and for what purposes the gods used the energy gate is something we can only guess at. Probably they used them when it was a question of conveying single individuals swiftly and without the help of spaceships from one place in the cosmos to another. This technique does not appear to have been perfected; there are a large number of legends according to which men, gods and demigods were often abruptly 'transferred' to distant and inhospitable parts of the Universe to which they were not meant to go at all.[10,11]

Were they 'industrial accidents'? That, too, must remain conjecture.

In any case, people are left with an inexplicable dread of all these things, particularly of gates and doors of any kind, and this was thoroughly exploited by the magician-priests in later times. While the sun gate of Tiahuanaco still seems to be more or less what one might imagine the transport installation plant required for this technique to be—just a gate without fore- or background—imagination already began to run wild in Egypt. There, outside the temple gate, are found whole avenues of Sphinxes, while outside the entrance squatted gigantic stone guards (possibly copies of humanoid robots or living overseers) to frighten away intruders. The wish to impress people by this means becomes apparent, for no danger could in fact threaten anyone who passed through these gates. After all, buildings made of stone, however impressive they may seem, are not machines, nor do they discharge energy.

The extensive scope of the dread-of-gates programming can be seen to this very day. The bridegroom protectively carrying his bride across the threshold (provided he has sufficient strength to do so!) does so not because of any popular tradition, but from this very dread of gates.

And a man passing through some hoary old castle or church gate who cannot refrain from shuddering even slightly—as though there might be something eerie lurking behind it—may well carry in his subconscious the remains of the knowledge, or perhaps even of the biological hereditary factors, of the gods who would have been thoroughly familiar with the risks and dangers connected with certain doorways.

It is interesting to note that this dread of gates, so deeply rooted in the subconscious, invariably relates only to *artificial* edifices and gates—a clear reference to the origin and development of this phobia. The cave dwellers did not have it, neither can it be found in the Eskimoes who lived far from the former residences of the gods, and thus from their 'gateway to heaven'.

In other parts of the world, however, one may encounter dozens of variations on the magic and mysticism of thresholds across doors or gates. For the ancient Germans, for instance, the threshold was sacred, while in villages, even to this day, peasants at the turn of the year will paint the initials of the three saints Caspar, Melchior and Balthazar, on the lintel above their front door.

The Old Testament tells how Jacob set up a stone where he had seen the ladder into heaven, saying: 'This is none other but the house of God, and this is the gate of heaven.' (Gen. 28:17-18)

After the exodus from Egypt, when Moses erected the first holy tabernacle, 'all the people saw the cloudy pillar stand at the tabernacle door: and all the people rose up and worshipped, every man in his tent door.' (Exod. 33:10)

And the prophet Ezekiel demanded: 'And the prince shall enter by the way of the porch of *that* gate without, and shall stand by the post of the gate . . . and he shall worship at the threshold of the gate . . .'. (Ezek. 46:2)

In none of these ancient Jewish writings, some of which go back to much earlier sources, do we find descriptions of the 'functioning' of such doors, thresholds and passages, although there are a few characteristic features:

> *The holy gates leading into heaven were taboo even for high dignitaries; only the priests and the initiated, who were the human assistants of the supposed gods, were allowed to tend and serve them.*

Sometimes the gates were filled with 'clouds' (as mentioned in Exodus). This translation of the Hebrew word is perhaps not quite accurate: it would be better to refer to 'fluttering' or 'a fluttering movement'. For it is a sombre fluttering and flickering which conveys that optical effect which one could expect, according to analogous physical rules, in connection with the discharge of higher forms of energy.

And what is one to think of the mysterious words of the prophet Amos (Amos 5:10) who, talking of man with reference to 'the Lord', abruptly and without any connection remarks: 'They hate him that rebuketh in the gate'?

Who is rebuked, or punished, in which gate, and why?

Amos offers no explanation. What is mentioned here (although the Jewish prophet who obviously adopted fragments of earlier traditions was not, of course, aware of this) is probably the already-mentioned danger in connection with certain gates: whoever does not know and observe the instructions to the letter will have to bear the consequences!

Connections with and references to gates are everywhere: Mary, the mother of Jesus, was honoured and celebrated in song as *ianua coeli* ('the door of heaven'), while the word *ianua* ('door') is in turn related to the ancient god Janus of the two faces, whose cult spread throughout Africa and Europe.

Janus had two faces: one of them gazed into our world, the other into a world unknown. In Rome he was known as 'door-keeper of heaven and master of the gate';[12] he had authority over all the doors and thoroughfares of the Roman Empire. In times of peace his temple in the Forum was closed, but in wartime the gates were opened so that the dead might have unhindered passage to the next world.[13]

The indirect successor of Janus was the apostle Peter who, as the pagan god before him, was given a 'staff' and the keys to the gates of heaven as emblems of his power.

Even in political linguistic usage the gate survives; the designation of 'The Sublime Porte' for the government of Turkey under the Sultans may go back to some historical origins, and yet the use of this concept demonstrates that subliminal feelings played a part in its choice.

Why, by the way, does modern psychology use the term 'subliminal'? Where does it originate? Quite simply, it comes from the imaginative world of our ancestors who believed that under the threshold (Latin *limen*) of the gate which ruled them demons and evil spirits were held spell-bound.[14]

Behind this seemingly nonsensical superstition there appears to be, upon logical consideration, nothing but a very remote memory of the fact that the technology of the gods involved negative and dangerous possibilities which (as with the energy gates) were normally under control, and thus 'spell-bound', and yet potentially present. This corresponds precisely with today's technique—with, perhaps, the difference that we do not master it nearly so well.

We have already briefly looked at the different purposes for which those gates and energy openings of the gods may have been used, marvelled at in tremulous reverence as they must have been by the people of those days, and later copied in a clumsy fashion: they were used for zero-time transport of persons (and objects) over vast cosmic distances.

In this context it may be assumed—in accordance with all the technical and theoretical considerations—that this system was dependent on the existence of counter-gates (i.e. receivers) at their place of destination; dependent also on other preconditions, as, for instance, a certain capacity for producing and discharging energy. Otherwise there would have been no need for the alternative of space travel by spaceship, which existed just as indubitably.

It is only to us that these things appear incredible. It is likely that the gods thought them lacking in perfection in the same way that today's motorist might regard his car, which may not always take him to his destination either.

It would appear that the principle of actual bodily ascension and transformation (and not only of mere disappearance and reappearance through the gates) with the help of furnaces, pits and sepulchres, rested on quite a different basis.

And if in this instance it was energies of a higher

dimension, not yet physically intelligible to us, that played a decisive part, they did so for a different purpose. As is evident from relevant traditions and reports, they were used to bring about a partial transformation of the material body, a state in which the person concerned was able to move freely in what was probably a restricted area, albeit partly independent of time and space, and dependent on his own will.

The technical 'how' can be reconstructed only in theory, although at the same time the facts taken from what, in this case, are most precise and concrete traditions from all over the world, do roughly indicate the general direction.

Is it at all possible to consider a 'semi-disembodiment' *not involving physical death?*

In a scientific and highly interesting investigation of the phenomenon of ball-lightning,[15] Professor R. Mühleisen of Esslingen, in a German scientific journal which is acknowledged as a serious publication, comes to the conclusion that this unusual and so far unexplained natural phenomenon must be a plasmoid state of electrical energy which cannot be re-created experimentally, but which does in fact exist.

The deduction by analogy, therefore, would be thus: if there are such intermediate states of energy, then there are probably similar states of matter. As yet they have no name, and we propose to call them (the concept is formulated here for the first time) *mesoity* ('intermediate existence').

This mesoity would correspond to an unstable and not easily maintained balance (as is the case, for a brief period, with ball-lightning) between a material space—time condition and a superordinate state.

Expressed in scientific terms: it would correspond to a pure energy field with only a partial material substratum; expressed in simple terms: it is water which is no longer liquid and not yet steam; or: still fluid yet already half--frozen. It is not easy to define it as one or the other or, above all, to recognize it.

How hard, then, it must have been for the followers of Jesus to identify their resurrected and half-transformed lord and master!

Mary Magdalene, the first to see him at the sepulchre, took him for a gardener: '. . . and knew not that it was Jesus.' (John 20:14)

The eleven (after the suicide of Judas) disciples fared no better. Two of them met him while they were out walking, 'but their eyes were holden that they should not know him.' (Luke 24:16) Only at night, when he sat at table with them breaking bread, 'their eyes were opened' (Luke 24:31), but at once he vanished from their sight.

According to the Gospels of Luke and John, Christ subsequently appeared to the disciples several times, displaying strange qualities on each occasion: first he passes through closed doors and walls, so that to begin with they take him to be a ghost (John 20: 19 and Luke 24: 37); then again he eats fish, honey and bread with them, like a normal person (Luke 24:42-3), and allows 'faithless' Thomas to touch the wound in his side (John 20:27).

This continues for weeks until his final ascension when he indicates to his disciples that he will return later (as did Quetzalcoatl to the Toltecs)— and this return, in both cases, has not taken place so far.

To avoid misunderstandings: the quotations cited above are not meant to prove the historic reality of Jesus of Nazareth. The point at issue here is solely the description of the ascension as well as the transformation in the Gospels.

Many modern theologians take the easy way out: although they declare these reports correctly to have been taken over from pagan religious belief,[16] they take that same belief to be fancy and invention.

But why should the pagans merely have indulged in fancy?

Whatever it was that the authors of the Christ legends took over from earlier cults and myths, it was neither invention nor fancy in the original either, but a recollection of even earlier events. As historical personalities Bel-Marduk, Tammuz and other gods of transformation and ascension were just as 'genuine' as Jesus Christ. They too were already imitations of originals that had not existed for hundreds or thousands of years. Most certainly the Gospels are a hotch-potch of all kinds of traditions—but basically they are not composed of falsehoods.

For that reason the popular assertion that physical resurrection is a fairy-tale because the life of Jesus Christ may perhaps have been one too, is as wrong as if one were to assert that because all the originals had been lost, there never was either a Rembrandt or a Titian, since there exist only copies of their paintings.

> *The person and the life of the saviour of the Christians are one thing; his resurrection, transformation and ascension as technological possibilities quite another.*
>
> *Christianity without resurrection may be inconceivable; resurrection without Christ is absolutely conceivable: it is probable and almost certain that it took place repeatedly long before his time.*

What remains of the 'originals', of actual resurrections and ascensions of gods, which lends itself to reconstruction today, since some 90 to 95 per cent of anything that may have been written in the past has been destroyed through man's stupidity and absurdity?

It is the Christ myth which offers most clues, since it is the most recent. From it the following characteristic features may be determined:

> *A demigod (son of God) who 'died' of his own free will is prepared in a special way and taken to a chamber or sepulchre.*
>
> *From this receptacle he re-emerges on the third (or fourth) day, strangely transformed and barely recognizable to those who have known him.*
>
> *In this state he can remain for some time, appear and disappear as he pleases, pass through walls, but at the same time take solid food and allow his body to be touched.*
>
> *Finally he ascends to heaven—as a person, and without technical equipment.*

In the course of these events, the sepulchre appears to play a decisive role, no matter whether it is called a grave, pit, furnace or even pyre. This could have been the transformation device.

Why else do both Luke (23:53) and John (19:39,41) place particular stress on the fact that the supposedly dead Christ, after special treatment by the enigmatic Nicodemus (in the other Gospels he is called Joseph) with mixtures and extracts of 'about an hundred pound weight', was placed in a rocky sepulchre 'wherein was never man yet laid'? And why was it those very men—the followers of Christ—who, from the allusions made by Jesus as well as from the words of the prophets, must have had at least an inkling of a possible resurrection, nevertheless covered the sepulchre with 'a great stone'? (Matt. 27:60; Mark 17:46) They hardly did this in order to prevent his resurrection, but rather for such a resurrection to be made possible at all!

Linked to the resurrection too is the 'earthquake' (Matt. 28:2) which took place after the burial of the Son of God, and following upon which the sepulchre was found open, its occupant having disappeared. According to the likely principles of higher-dimensional physics, disturbances in the space—time structure would have to be expected during the transformation of matter into a mesoic state—and there are, in fact, references to similar concomitant phenomena in other reports of resurrections.

Last but not least there is, in this context, one remarkable detail worth mentioning: in Mark, Luke and John mention is made of one or two angels who were supposedly seen in the empty sepulchre by the female members of the young sect, and to whom they actually spoke.

The official Church tries to get round these accounts by, at most, acknowledging them as 'spiritually symbolic', although they are more consistent and concrete than many other incidents in eyewitness reports on the life of Christ.

In Mark, for example, it is said of the women who came to the sepulchre on the third day after the execution of their spiritual leader: 'And entering into the sepulchre' (which, judging from that remark, must have been rather large) 'they saw a young man sitting on the right side, clothed in a long white garment; and they were affrighted. And he saith unto them, Be not affrighted: Ye seek Jesus of Nazareth, which was crucified: he is risen; he is not here.' (Mark 16: 5-6)

Luke describes the same scene thus: 'And they entered in, and found not the body of the Lord Jesus. And it came to pass, as they were much perplexed thereabout, behold, two men stood by them in shining garments: And as they were afraid, and bowed down *their* faces to the earth, they said unto them, Why seek ye the living among the dead? He is not here, but is risen.' (Luke 24: 3-6)

And in John too (30: 12-13) there are 'two angels in white' who ask Mary Magdalene: 'Woman, why weepest thou?' prior to her meeting the resurrected Jesus in person.

In literal translation and according to the concepts of those days, 'angels' (Greek *angeloi*) are nothing but messengers or announcers, and by no means what is understood by the word today. It is likely, then, that Luke refers to 'men' in his Gospel.

What did these messenger-men, whose 'shining' garments once again recall the Toltec legend of Teccucizctecatl and Nanahuatzin (who were also attired in 'iridescent' robes), have to do with Jesus and his resurrection?

Well, probably nothing at all with the resurrection of this demigod, which is not very likely to have taken place anyway, but presumably quite a lot with many earlier and real transformations.

Before the launching of spaceships in our century, men in white overalls are seen busily rushing about; these are the technicians, the helpers and assistants of the astronauts.

If after the launching one were to ask them where the vanished space travellers had gone, and if they were to reply in the archaic language of Bible translation, their answer would be something like: 'Why seek ye them here, they have been carried up into heaven . . .'.

And a member of the Watutsi tribe or an Amazon Indian would not understand that either, and regard the technicians in their white protective overalls as beings from another world.

The 'transformation technicians' of the gods—whose transformation techniques are still unknown to us—have been dead a long time, but their appearance must have been impressive enough for it still to crop up in the Gospels, with the result that they came to be honoured by being regarded as angels.

Basically these things have nothing to do with magic and sorcery; they became embarrassing superstitions only in the insufficiently enlightened minds of latter-day scientists and priests.

How clear and simple, in contrast, is the way in which John (20:17) lets the newly transformed Jesus say to Mary Magdalene: 'Touch me not!' (*Noli me tangere*). Why, when later he does eat and drink, allowing Thomas to touch his wound?

There is one reasonable explanation to which it would seem Jesus referred, even if he, or the author of this Gospel, no longer knew the reasons and historical connections:

> *Anyone who had just been 'resurrected' was presumably in a state where the balance of matter and energy was extremely unstable, and to be touched when in this condition might have been quite dangerous not only for him, but also for the other person.*

Perhaps a somewhat remote parallel may be drawn with the tests carried out by both the USA and the Soviet Union for the practical utilization of nuclear fusion energy, where it is vital that unstable matter is kept in a vacuum and, with the help of magnetic fields, is prevented from touching the walls of the reactors which would otherwise destroy it. Put in the simplest terms possible: a 'lump' of matter, superheated to millions of degrees and with its nuclei in fusion, is floating in a vacuum while being held together by strong magnetic fields—that is the picture presented by the American 'stellarator'.

As already mentioned, the comparison is a lame one; it is intended merely to show that there is a relationship in principle, and that in the final analysis all processes of resurrection and transformation are, or were, similarly based on the techniques used in physics.

It would appear that in the mesoic state of a biological body a stabilization (and thus a certain mobility) sets in after one or two days. This is mentioned in the Gospel of St Luke (24:31 and 24:40-2); Christ, appearing to two of his disciples on the very evening of his resurrection, exchanges only a few brief words with them and then disappears swiftly; only on the following day does he 'show' them his hands and feet and take nourishment.

What is most astonishing in the conduct ascribed to Jeshu of Nazareth is that it had been handed down *earlier*, and with scant change, for thousands of years.

Only in Christianity did it become an incomprehensible myth. And yet it would certainly be a mistake to believe that at the time when the gods practised the art of transformation, there were mysterious initiates who understood and took over its science and technology.

In reality, all backward-looking speculations apart, it was more likely that human eyewitnesses alive in those days understood precious little of any such proceedings. Indeed, how many persons of average education and intelligence are there today who could explain the function and technology of a computer which they may have seen a few times at their place of employment? The less reason for reproaching our ancestors who had only just (and probably not without assistance from the gods) evolved into human beings.

In certain respects, their inability to understand may even be a guarantee for the truth of their traditions:

> *Because they could not fathom what they were experiencing and observing, they recorded it without additions of their own, recording it in concepts familiar to them.*

Thus, for instance, the Southern Galla, a tribe on the east coast of Africa, report[17] a 'Wak Bird' which had come to them on behalf of the gods, and which had recommended that they should 'slough their skin', for they would then become immortal. Their forefathers, however, not understanding this piece of advice, remained mortal. The Dusum of north Borneo tell a similar tale. They too claim to have received a hint from the gods to slough their skins as snakes do, to gain immortality. But, so it would appear, they failed to pay due attention while receiving their instructions, and their quest for eternal life therefore came to nothing.

The memories of the Cashinava on the upper Amazon are even more distinct:[18] long ago, the father of their divine bringer of culture had taken his son and several human beings with him up to heaven, impressing upon the tribe beforehand to watch carefully for the moment when he would call out: 'Cast off your skin!' Unfortunately, so we are told, the Cashinava did not, or could not, do this, and thus they continued to be susceptible to death.

The (snake-) skin sloughing story promptly turns up again in Jewish-Christian mysticism. According to Jewish belief,[19] the sacred snake was identified with the expected Messiah; John (3:14) says of Christ: 'And as Moses lifted up the serpent in the wilderness, even so must the Son of man be lifted up', while the Christian Gnostics—the Ophites and Naassenes—depicted the Saviour as 'snake-shaped'.[20]

Snakes of all kinds—good ones and evil ones—play an important role in legends and religions. There exist entire libraries on the subject, and for several good reasons. One of these reasons, namely that connected with resurrection and transformation, may be interpreted comparatively easily. What we have to do is to imagine *how*, roughly, the primitive peoples of those days might have experienced the transformation and ascension of a god or gods. They must have been scenes of uncanny unfamiliarity, engraving themselves indelibly on the memory of the people.

After long preparations and ceremonies, one or two of the lords of the world who had come out of the cosmos, dressed in iridescent uniforms, walked slowly up to a chamber-like appliance which either stood on a raised platform or was sunk into the ground, and in front of which assistants, also dressed in white, were waiting.

A gate, up till then invisible, swung open and was carefully shut after the gods had passed through. All that the mortals, lying flat on their faces in fear and reverence and intoning some kind of chant, could see was a glow in the interior of the furnace or sepulchre as if a fire had been lit, and that the fastenings of the chamber were as solid as its walls.

After three or four days, after the earth had briefly rumbled and trembled, the gates opened again and the transformed gods stepped out: without their garments, shining from within and scarcely recognizable.

Thus, surrounded by a flickering and shining aura, they raised themselves from the ground, slowly, like air bubbles in water, and rose higher and higher: not in one of those round or pole-shaped vehicles which one would see standing around on mountains and smooth runways, or often racing up into the sky thundering and roaring—that had almost become an every-day event; and not by going through one of those strange gates, to dissolve into nothing inside them. This was something quite different.

It was possible to see clearly the men who had been bodily resurrected from their sepulchres; indeed, sometimes they even spoke to and with those standing next to them, before finally disappearing into the sky.

How else could those wretched Earth dwellers have recorded events of such magnitude other than by comparing them to nature, with which they were so much more familiar? They had no knowledge of physics and technology, but a snake sloughing its skin was something quite normal and could be observed anywhere. Thus they used this phenomenon in order to describe what they had seen and experienced: seemingly dead gods cast off their old 'skin' and, transformed, are carried up to the stars.

The supposition that what even in prehistoric times must have been a matter-of-course event—namely the casting of a snake's skin—should have stimulated people to invent whole mythologies, is complete nonsense, and could only have been created in the minds of nineteenth-century scholars who viewed nature 'with their backs to the window'. In reality, all snake cults and myths which are in any way connected with resurrection, transformation and ascension probably go back to memories of events like those outlined above.

Moreover, on closer investigation of the Cashinava legend the impression is created that the gods (or certain of their scientists) did actually try to let several inhabitants of the planet Earth join in both transformation and ascension. But it appears that the latter were neither physically nor spiritually capable of this feat. This path to immortality was inaccessible to them.

All the more touching are the attempts made by our forebears to copy their revered gods. Of course, they could not copy the manufactured machines and gadgets (as, for instance, the 'Oreichalkos'[21] of the gods, shimmering like gold), for they had only one stable material at their disposal—stone. They certainly had no sense of 'fine' differences, as long as the outward form roughly corresponded. This is why today we are puzzled by copies of archetypal originals, like the sun gate of Tiahuanaco, the narrow entrances of Egyptian temples, and, as a last and very faint allusion, the little 'cellulae' (small chambers) inside Greek temples which today can be found in the sacristies (or 'sacred rooms') behind the altars in Christian churches.

We find ourselves unable to discover the meaning and purpose of those cone-shaped and gateless circular towers of the ruined city of Zimbabwe in Rhodesia, or of the almost identical 'Nuraghen' in Sardinia, while in France[22] there are quite solid buildings of the same nature and form which have been interpreted by imaginative authors as mysterious 'places of initiation'. From the time of the Pharaohs of Egypt to the Middle Ages we stand before sepulchres, rock tombs and sarcophagi which were never meant to be real graves ('. . . wherein was never man yet laid . . .') and which represent a certain tradition only in the exact correspondence of ir dimensions:

> It is probable that none of these are relics of the gods, nor do they in any way possess magic qualities; they are primitive, and thus ineffectual, imitations, just like a child's ships, cars and castles made out of sand.

The models no longer exist; they have vanished, been

removed or destroyed, and there is no temple or church in the world where we shall ever see that power again which once worked the installations of the gods, enabling them to practise transformation and ascension.

What has remained are dead stones and cults based on what has been handed down at second, third and fourth hand. There also remains some instinctive feeling that there once was a time when these things—the ascensions of the gods, their energy-transportation gates, their transformation chambers and furnaces—did exist.

Physical transformation was probably only one of several methods used. As yet we cannot quite understand its method of working, but it would seem that it was not used very often. Why that was so is discussed in another chapter.

The 'resurrection in the flesh' which has assumed so much significance for the West, must be ascribed to Christianity, which has made this variant—taken from Near Eastern myths—the focal point of its belief. Why it had been preserved so actively there of all places (and later played no particular role at all in other parts of the world) is still a question for historians.

> To repeat once more and as plainly as possible: physical transformation, resurrection and ascension appear to have existed at some time or other. However, since the disappearance of the gods it has hardly ever been practised, quite simply because the technological preconditions necessary were lacking.

Whatever the names of later gods of resurrection—Quetzalcoatl, Bel-Marduk, Dionysus or Christ—and no matter whether they actually existed or not, none of them was able to rise in the sense in which the gods practised this. Theirs are names (and perhaps in one or two cases even persons) which have been linked with historical facts.

It is true that for thousands of years priestly as well as ruling castes have taken advantage of the effect exerted by such mythologies on people who, through the processes of heredity and distant memories, were preprogrammed. In

25

contrast to such myths, an attempt (most conscientious and based solely on logical and causal criteria) has been made here to reveal likely connections and to trace apparent enigmas back to their reasonable and intelligible origins.

Long-established religions are now gradually dying off; for their adherents physical resurrection is either merely unintelligible and obscure dogma, or even embarrassment (as it is for many Protestants). We have, however, in our search from magic back to knowledge, come to the conclusion that this resurrection was a genuine reality—and could be so once again: not as some nebulous promise for Judgment Day, but as a problem to be solved scientifically. Whether in principle it is worth striving for is quite a different matter.

2 Gods and men

At the beginning of June 1972, the news agencies announced (*Kurier*, Vienna, 3 June):

'According to a report by the American Academy of Science the existence of extra-terrestrial intelligences is "most probable". The Academy's Committee for Astronomy has therefore demanded an increase in the relevant research funds from 390 to 488 million dollars. In the Academy's 129-page report on the probability of extra-terrestrial life, we read, among others: "Perhaps at this very moment, and through this very document, there flow radio waves containing the conversations of living beings far away . . ."

'In order to prove the existence of intelligences outside our solar system as soon as possible, US scientists demand the allocation and erection of still more powerful telescopes, and of other scientific apparatus.'

Despite such announcements there are still people who think that the wave of interest in the gods, started by the Swiss Erich von Däniken a few years ago (and which in actual fact goes back to discoveries and theories of Russian scholars), will subside like any other. They could turn out to be wrong.

The existence of extra-terrestrial intelligences and the likelihood of their having visited Earth on several occasions and changed the course of history, tend to throw into doubt those fundamentals of history, biology, technology and philosophy which up to now have been considered irrefutable and suggest the necessity for complete rethinking in many

27

fields.

> *I propose that without the presence and influence of the gods on Earth there would have been no evolution of man nor anything of what we call religion—no Osiris, no Zeus, no Buddha and no Christ.*

We must now find out who these gods were, how they came to our planet and what they wanted here.

How they overcame distances of unimaginable light years (for they could not have come from our solar system) is a physical and technological problem which the author discussed in detail in his book *Heimkehr zu den Göttern*, 1971. They may have travelled in faster-than-light spaceships, and later they probably mastered 'inter-cosmic traffic' with the help of energy transport gates as well as partial matter-transformers.

However, the point at issue is the *real consequence* of their temporary presence for our history, present and future. There is, for example, a question of the utmost importance for our spiritual and religious life, which ought to be answered: why should these mysterious cosmic beings have resembled human beings and not, say, fish or insects—or something altogether different. The answer is startlingly simple:

> *The gods do not (or did not) look like us because we imagine them like that, but because, in all probability, they fashioned us after their likeness.*

In Genesis (1:27) it says clearly and simply: 'So God created man in his *own* image, in the image of God created he him.' To deduce from this statement that a supreme spiritual entity (i.e. God) would have hands, feet and ears like ours, would be as ingenuous as trying to find some hidden mystical meaning in these words. Whatever they say, they say clearly and unambiguously: a god (or gods) rigged up, bred or fashioned in some way or other, a human prototype after his (or their)

28

own biological form.

This does not indicate that there may not be other intelligent beings in the Universe which look totally different.

> *Had it been reptile-like beings who first landed on Earth, perhaps we should now look more like lizards than men.*

There are no definitive rules whereby intelligence must be linked to a specific bodily shape.

Admittedly, according to the very plausible conjectures of biologists and palaeontologists (Driesch, Klaatsch, Daqué, Professor Sauser and others) the human shape does *seem* to be the most suited to its purpose, but that opinion is not absolutely inviolable. Men did, and do, proudly regard their shape as sacred principally because it has originated from the gods. There is not one civilized people that does not trace its origin back to the gods—as, for instance, the Japanese or the Goths. [1]

There are echoes of the 'paternity' of the gods even in the New Testament. After the baptism of Jesus by John the Baptist, a voice from heaven was heard to say: 'This is my beloved Son, in whom I am well pleased.' (Matt. 3:17) Jesus makes many similar statements about himself, as in Luke 22:70 when questioned by the high priests: 'Then said they all, Art thou then the Son of God? And he said unto them, Ye say that I am.'

It would appear, though, that to begin with this state of men being the children of God was not altogether an ideal one; there are enough reports to suggest that the gods eliminated errors in breeding ruthlessly and brutally. This emerges clearly not only in the story of the flood; the Bambala, a negro tribe in the Congo, recount [2] that a former human race was destroyed by the gods because they had been disobedient and useless. 'Many and different annihilations of mankind have taken place and will take place in the future,' states the Greek philosopher Plato in his 'Timaeus' (22/23).

The legendary Yeti, the Abominable Snowman who is said to roam the Tibetan mountains (the Nepalese historian

Narnathi Nath claimed to have seen him in July 1972)—is he the relic of a human breed that went wrong?

Why did the gods create man at all? The Sumerians and other peoples claim it was 'so that he might bear the burden of creation',[3] or to put it in simple terms: so that he might look after them and serve them, as a slave, as a biological robot.

Naturally, there were slave riots in consequence. There is a report in an ancient Babylonian cuneiform text from the time of Hammurabi[4] which tells that in prehistoric days the 'Igigi', the servants of the gods, had risen against them after a long period of forced labour; they were promptly annihilated after they had dared to threaten Enlil, the 'Lord of the Atmosphere', in his own palace at Nippur.

> One is free to think what one likes about these and other traditional legends, but one thing surely stands out as odd: if men had in fact invented their own history, is it likely that they would have represented themselves as creatures and slaves of the gods and as lords of the Earth from the very beginning?

Moreover, comparatively white-skinned people, like the Sumerians and the Babylonians, would hardly have described the first men as 'black-heads' or remarked that they had reddish-brown skins[5] (the meaning of 'Adam' is after all nothing other than 'red', or 'made of red clay'.)[6] It would appear that in prehistoric times the white-coloured skin (and the 'blue blood' too) were the privilege of the gods; men were red or black.

A further question: Why did the gods come to Earth at all? Here we have no other source but legends and traditions. They vary from nation to nation as well as in their details, but they have a common core:

In the remote past, a 'lord of worlds' (he is known variously as Uranus, Vishnu, Brahma, Sido and by dozens of other names) ruled on a planet in the centre of our Galaxy (Milky Way). He sent expeditions to the 'lower worlds' (this may be a concept from earlier astronaut slang), which seemed to include our solar system.

It is not certain whether this was an undertaking of a military and scientific nature, or the banishment of beings who, for some reason, had become *persona non grata*—the 'fallen angels' of Revelation. Neither is it certain whether there was more than one wave of colonization by extra-terrestrial forces.

If one goes back to earliest sources, one comes across references to the effect that, before the arrival of the first strangers, the Earth was 'without form, and void' (Gen. 1:2)—indeed, even without oxygen in its atmosphere. This is fact, not fancy.[7] Before plants began to cover the Earth, its atmosphere consisted predominantly of methane, ammonia, carbon dioxide, hydrogen cyanide and other gases favouring the development of organic life (or its reproduction from 'imported' cosmic seeds). For this first kind of life on Earth, the oxygen which the plants produced as waste product was poison. It had to adapt itself or perish. All present organic forms are, in this sense, survivors of the great oxygen disaster. Recent experiments have confirmed this: most plants thrive better in a mixture of air containing only half (10 instead of 21 per cent) the normal proportion of oxygen; they therefore suffer in their own waste gas production (which, however, is vital for us).

After the soft landing of the Russian space probe *Venus 8* in July 1972, consideration was given to the possibility of changing some of the atmosphere on Venus (which consists of 95 per cent carbon dioxide) into oxygen by means of 'injections' of blue algae cultures while, at the same time, gradually lowering both high atmospheric pressure (900 atmospheres absolute pressure) and high surface temperature (450°C). In this way, according to the calculations of Soviet scientists, men could land and live on Venus in about 600 years. When one reads and hears such things, it no longer seems irrelevant to assume that the gods may have done something similar with Earth.

Esoteric Egyptian doctrines[8] tell that four archetypal gods 'raised the sun'. Presumably this means that it was they who took the Earth to its present position, while previously it had been in darkness. This crops up in many legends, even of tribes quite cut off from the rest of the world, like the Songhai in the Sudan.[9]

Utopic? Fanciful? In 1971 the American astronomer, Dr S. Singer, proposed in all seriousness that the smaller of the two moons of Mars, Deimos, which has a diameter of only a few kilometres, should be thrown off course through controlled atomic explosions and made to rotate round the Earth where it would then be possible to study it closely.

There should be no doubt that the gods had at their disposal better means than atom bombs.

If one reads the first seventeen or eighteen verses of the creation in the Bible (Gen. 1:1-18), interpreting it in a different way from students of the Bible, the following facts may be noticed:

In succession God first creates light (1:3), then he forms the Earth and lets 'grass, the herb . . . *and* the fruit tree yielding fruit' (1:11) grow on it; only then (1:14-18) does he set the 'lights' (sun, moon and stars) in the sky. Beasts and man come much later.

According to this sequence, then, Earth had plants as well as a certain cycle of day and night, *before* the sun and the moon began to shine.

> *In consequence there would have been an Earth which, to begin with, was lit not by the sun but only by 'light'; this is precisely what other traditions say: the planet Earth floated in some kind of twilight until the gods came and got 'a place in the sun' for it!*

It would be illogical to look upon the story of the creation as poetic invention, for then God would have made the heavenly bodies appear together with (or before) Earth. Genesis, however, is not a work of poetry, as some modern-thinking theologians have lately conceived it to be, but a factual report in fragments, and in this sense clear and logical. It must be considered that in its entire development the Earth may have been significantly 'manipulated' by intelligent and purposeful powers, even though we may not know details for a long time to come. A significant error committed by Bible translators, and initiated by Martin Luther, must be corrected: At the beginning of the Holy Scripture it is not written 'In the beginning God created the heaven and the earth', but '. . . the gods created the heaven and the earth'.

The Hebrew text at this point expressly refers to 'Elohim', which is a plural word; elsewhere (whenever God is mentioned), the word Jehovah (JHVH) is used exclusively—a kind of camouflage name for the supreme deity, since it was strictly forbidden to pronounce or write his real name. Even according to this account, then, it was by no means a Jewish tribal god who created the Earth, but godlike beings who used an already existing installation and converted it for their own purposes. When they did this, and how, we do not know. After all, recent conjectures and calculations show the age of the Earth to be not three or four, but ten or eleven thousand million years old (according to the Russian professor Erich Gerlin, in *Sputnik*, 7/1969, Stuttgart), and whatever we know of its history has so far been pure theorizing.

There is one thing which, on the basis of all existing traditions, we may regard as probable: those gods who were our physical or artificial forefathers, and from whom originates practically all we possess by way of knowledge and religion, do not appear to have been the first visitors to Earth but the *most recent*.

They no longer found the Earth 'without form, and void', but habitable to some extent—as Mirtlok, the 'middle world', as the Indians called it, or Midgard, the 'middle garden' of the ancient Germans.[10]

In this 'garden' lived groups of half-men, and also Titans, Cyclops or Asurs—presumably descendants of earlier colonizing waves, for they possessed a fairly highly developed technology with flying vehicles and energy weapons; they were defeated by the 'young gods',[11] and subsequently either banished to inhospitable worlds or forced to collaborate. An echo of this can still be found in the legends of those incredibly skilled 'smiths'—from Hephaestus through Daedalus to Mime and Wieland (who had to do forced labour, and in most cases took cruel revenge).

The people of that time do not seem to have liked the 'old gods', the Titans, very much. They were coarse and vicious and kept themselves to themselves, which is why the newly-landed occupying forces from the Universe (like the Americans in 1945) were welcomed as liberators; from then on the Titans were considered wicked.[12]

The new masters of the world held out a promise (as did those of 1945) of paradise: progress, peace, prosperity. They may or may not have kept this promise.

They taught the people many things, including a minimum of moral behaviour and order, and supposedly also bringing them a number of useful animals and plants, such as maize.

'Maize is a phenomenon', states Karl F. Kohlenberg in his *Enträtselte Vorzeit*, referring to statements by botanists and historians:[13] 'What distinguishes the maize plant from all other types of grain is its biological helplessness. Left to itself, it would very quickly die out. Its seeds sit so firmly beneath the husk that no wind could scatter them. Should a forgotten ear of maize fall to the ground, then, though the seeds may produce hundreds of seedlings, they nevertheless grow in such thick clumps that none of them is able to develop normally.'

The Aztecs thought that both man and the maize plant were star-born, sharing a common celestial home; with many peoples there remains a memory of their divine instructors who taught them the basic principles of agriculture. For the Chinese this is the demigod Shen-nung,[14] for the Melanesians the god Quat[15] and for the Greeks, and the Romans, the goddesses Demeter and Ceres.

No less baffling, and so far not satisfactorily explained, is the question of how the seedless banana has managed to spread across half the Earth.

That certain plants and animals should not have originated on Earth seems surprising and almost unbelievable only at first glance. After all, there are similar or related stones and minerals on the moon and on Mars; organic life must have developed in the same way on any planet which is habitable as we understand it.

In the same way it is difficult to understand why, over huge areas of the Earth, men should suddenly turn from being hunters and nomads as they had been for hundreds of thousands of years and become tillers of the soil. Who was it that gave them the impetus?

In 1920 the Russian poet and philosopher Valerij Bryusov wrote: 'The origins of cultures so widely differing and so dispersed geographically as the Aegean, Egyptian, Babylonian, Etruscan, Indian, Aztec and Pacific, display similarities which cannot be explained solely by the borrowings of one people from another and by imitation. One ought to look beyond antiquity for an "unknown factor" which set the machine going which we know today. The Egyptians, the Babylonians, the Greeks and the Romans were our teachers. But who taught the teachers?'

Today, when the consciousness of our link with the cosmos begins to stir once more, one might reply to Bryusov by saying that that unknown factor, those teachers, were the gods.

Admittedly, this development aid of theirs was not altruistic, but rather pragmatic-egotistical.

'Let us create a being which is obedient and faithful, which feeds and keeps us . . .'; thus spoke the Maya gods Tzakól, Bitól, Gucumatz and others.[16] Thus they had promptly established the 'political line' of their work on Earth: men were civilized insofar as it was expedient, but not more than necessary. They were trained for farming and stockbreeding, and settled in communes round the seats of the gods, which is probably the origin of the 'city'. Most of the oldest cities known to us were created round the 'sanctuary' of a 'town god', as was the above-mentioned Nippur (today: Nuffar), centre of the Sumerian chief god Enlil, from whom the rulers of all the other cities of Mesopotamia derived their authority. 'In prehistoric times man and beast, plants and land, and all earthly possessions were the property of the town god and thus of his representative on earth, the priest-king', wrote Wolf Schneider in his monograph on the nature of towns.[17]

It would appear that, at least initially, 'no fraternization' was the order of the day for the gods (as it has always been for occupying forces); their dwellings and their plants were absolutely out of bounds to most men.

At the same time, however, it is certain that the longer the gods stayed on Earth the more blatantly their 'race laws' were broken. In Genesis 6:2 this is stated quite plainly: 'That the sons of God saw the daughters of men, that they *were* fair; and they took them wives of all which they chose.'

The practice of the slogan 'Frau komm!'* seems to have been the usual thing even in those days. Despite their incredible technical and scientific superiority, the men from another star (and, incidentally, the ladies too, of which more later) behaved in many respects humanly—indeed, only too humanly!

It would be wrong, therefore, to see them as supernatural and lofty beings; it is only men's imagination which has thus portrayed them, an imagination which has always taken semblance for substance, worshipping every power—so long as it is in power.

In reality the gods were not very different from us, for after all, we are more or less their direct descendants. Moreover, as all traditions suggest, they proved themselves true men by their moral attitudes: as helpers, heroes and benefactors—and as mass murderers, gangsters and bandits.

This is illustrated by the discovery made by our original parent, Adam, whose first wife Lilith (whom he married before Eve) is said to have been a Titaness, i.e. a member of the former ruling caste on Earth.[18] On account of her ancestry she was continually slandered by both divine and human propaganda agencies of the past. It was said that she had used fatal magic words,[19] and that she had stolen the 'Golden Tablets of Fate' from the gods (perhaps some kind of programming foil for their machines).

How effective this slander was can be gathered from Persian-Arabic mythology:[20] Adam, we read, after his sepa-

* This refers to the practice of the Russians in Berlin of accosting women and girls before forcibly taking them away.

ration from Lilith and his fall with Eve, was punished by God by having to spend another 130 years in exile with his wicked first wife—only then was he allowed to return to Eve. Diabolical rather than divine punishment for a married man who had been divorced and had remarried!

All in all, it was a well-thought-out propaganda campaign which, after they had assumed power, the young gods carried out against their predecessors the Titans, Asurs or whatever they are to be called. The ancient Greeks still reported with a shudder that Dionysus, Zeus's son, had been dismembered and torn to pieces by the Titans.[21] They were represented as ugly, misshapen and leaden-skinned and they lived at the Schwarzalfenheim of the ancient Germans,[22] a bleak, cold world from where they are said to have come to Earth.

As always, human beings joined in the persecution and tormenting—forgetting, as they did so, that it was a Titan, Prometheus, who had brought them the gift of fire and who had pleaded for them when Zeus had once again wanted to destroy them.[23]

The propaganda machine of the gods and their successors functioned most efficiently, reprogramming Prometheus-Lucifer, the light-bringer, to become a demon. In this case, as well as in general, it would appear that the 'de-Titanizing' of prehistoric times was hardly distinguishable from the racist, religious and ideological purges of our immediate past and present.

Woe betide anyone who resisted these proceedings! The gods were merciless and ruthlessly used every means at their disposal: 'And I will destroy your high places, and cut down your images and cast your carcasses upon the carcasses of your idols, and my soul shall abhor you. And I will make your cities waste, and bring your sanctuaries unto desolation, and I will not smell the savour of your sweet odours [this presumably refers to the odour of corpses].' Thus Moses (Lev. 26:30-1) allows his god to reprove the followers of the previous masters and gods.

These were not merely empty words, as is testified by the prophet Isaiah (37:36): 'Then the angel of the LORD went forth and smote in the camp of the Assyrians a hundred and fourscore and five thousand; and when they [the Israelites] arose early in the morning, behold, they *were* all dead corpses.' One hundred and eighty-five thousand at one blow: there were only a few more at Hiroshima.

There are 'dead corpses' in the Old Testament (following punitive expeditions of the gods) by the hundred thousand. The fact that the redoubtable Martin Luther was not seized by doubt and dread when he was busy translating these horror stories can be explained only when one recalls that, in his day too, human life was not valued very highly; but the fact that these bloodthirsty tales are proclaimed as 'Holy Writ' even today is the affair of those who do so.

This may be seen as confirmation of the brutal consistency with which the gods liquidated their enemies; it is also an interesting hint at the origin of the well-known intolerance of Christianity which has even found expression in the words of that supposedly most peaceloving of men, Jeshu of Nazareth (Mark 16:16): 'He that believeth and is baptized shall be saved; but he that believeth not shall be damned.'

Is that an expression of the Son of Man's much-praised love for mankind? No, it is the curse of a son of the gods (and a welcome excuse for all subsequent Christian mass-murderers in history): whoever disobeys shall go to the devil! Already in the pre-Christian religion of the ancient Persians [24] blasphemers and other nonconformists were damned and sent to hell.

How typical of the gods' mentality! Since they were in a way themselves banished, they threatened anyone who disobeyed them with banishment and damnation. It is likely that they did not think of a hell of the Catholic kind, complete with vats of boiling oil and a sea of flames, but rather of unlovely planets of which there were, and still are, plenty.

Control over these unattractive regions of the cosmos was, of course, passed on by the gods to the Titans. Hel, who is said to have been mistress of nine such sunless and uncomfortable heavenly bodies, was a Titaness and one of the daughters of Loki, the ancient German bringer of light.[25] In those days to be banished to Hel—to hell—must have been as bad as to Siberia in Czarist or Stalinist Russia.

These, however, are merely harmless and entertaining comparisons and stories. It would be amusing, for example, to discover that in Revelation (9:11) the Greek god of light, Apollo, has turned into a prince of hell, an 'angel of the bottomless pit', were it not that those stories were the basis for that belief in devils, hell and demons and for its later disastrous consequences—indeed, for that somewhat dubious and ambiguous morality of Christianity and other religions.

It is becoming increasingly apparent that almost everything that the religions (which in the most literal sense of the word are nothing but links with what the gods had asserted and explained) proclaim to be 'good' and 'evil', has hardly anything to do with our ideas in this respect. What they were concerned with first and foremost was their power and their domination—what was useful in this respect was 'good'; what seemed to be detrimental was 'evil'.

None other than the most Christian Saviour of Christianity says so emphatically in Luke 19:27: 'But those mine enemies, which would not that I should reign over them, bring hither, and slay *them* before me.' ('And when he had thus spoken, he went before, ascending up to Jerusalem.' (Luke 19:28))

Verily, verily, a fine God of Love. . . .

One should not be angry with the historic Jesus, half rabbi, half revolutionary, because of what he said: he probably never said it anyway, just as he never said at least 90 per cent of what was later ascribed to him. Those sayings are 'words of the gods', just like all those speeches that thunder of judgment and the dreadful punishment of the wicked who would not obey the gods.

'Then shall he say also unto them on the left hand, Depart from me, ye cursed, into everlasting fire, prepared for the devil and his angels.' (Matt. 25:41) 'And these shall go away into everlasting punishment: but the righteous into life eternal.' (Matt. 25:46)

Who were these righteous who were not damned like those

standing on the left? They were the satraps and servants of the new masters, 'made . . . kings and priests' (Rev. 1:6) and empowered to rule the heathens as well as to exterminate them as they chose. 'And he that overcometh, and keepeth my works unto the end, to him will I give power over the [heathen] nations: And he shall rule them with a rod of iron; as the vessels of a potter shall they be broken to shivers.' (Rev. 2:26-7) That is the message which the alleged spirit of Christ has asked John of Patmos to deliver to the community at Thyarita. On which occasion the loving son of God remarks casually: 'And I will kill her children with death. . . .' (Rev. 2:23)

According to the Redeemer's own words (Matt. 5:3) it was, among others, those 'poor in spirit' who would escape such massacres—and they, of course, were unable to cause trouble for the gods. Those who were to be rewarded were the willing helpers and servants, as Isaiah promises: '. . . but he that putteth his trust in me shall possess the land, and shall inherit my holy mountain.' (Isaiah 57:15)

Whether this promise of him who 'dwells in the high and holy *place*' is to be taken altogether seriously is, admittedly, doubtful when one supposes that the 'holy mountains' concealed the gods' starting, landing and transformation installations.

Considered from a modern viewpoint, all these threats and promises recall occupying forces needing and seeking help and assistance because they are not sure where they stand. They too make wild promises to the collaborators and threaten those who resist with all the tortures of hell.

The gods appear to have been in just such a situation, for the former gods and rulers whom they had driven out (the Titans and Asurs) were by no means dead and finished, but lived and fought on—the 'tupamaros' of prehistoric times, with changing fortunes and for thousands of years. And, in spite of their bad reputation, they still had followers here and there. Even today the Yasids (they call themselves the Davasin) in Kurdistan worship Satan as the true lord of the Earth.[26] They call him Melek Ta'us (King Peacock). He seems to have been some kind of underground fighter after the style of Ché Guevara, for in the holy book of the Yasids (the *Kitab Asvad* ('Black Book')) he says to his companions: 'You shall not call me by my name . . . for you know not the truth; worship me only in my symbol and my image.'

This is routine secret service jargon. Thus Stalin (whose name was Djugashvili) and Tito (Josip Broz) were and are known only by their pseudonyms. Melek Ta'us, that Robin Hood of remote antiquity, the first-born son of the incorporeal supreme god, had, so the Yasids believe, a genuine claim to the Earth:[27] he was the 'prince of this world', a title by which even Christians still acknowledge the devil.

Actually we are never really told quite why this position is supposed to be so wicked and evil: and it would be impossible to do so.

> *The deeper one penetrates into prehistory the clearer one thing becomes: In all the stories and traditions about the fight for the rulership of the world, it is not a question of a moral struggle between good and evil as we understand them, but of a struggle for power by cliques of gods.*

Echoes of these struggles are still to be found in the New Testament and in that body of Christian belief which for two thousand years has influenced, and influences still, our history and attitudes.

This becomes particularly clear when one considers the concept of grace: in it is manifested the absolute arbitrariness of the gods who reward and punish as the whim takes them.

'Then shall two be in the field: the one shall be taken, and the other left', Matthew (24:40) writes literally. The one who actually says these words is Jesus of Nazareth and it is interesting to note that when he said it he was sitting on a 'mountain' (Matt. 5:1), that is to say, on what was certainly a place of residence and proclamation of the gods. And at his first mass meeting ('. . . and there followed him great multitudes', Matt. 4:25) he said something else very strange: 'For I say unto you, That except your righteousness shall exceed *the righteousness* of the scribes and Pharisees, ye shall in no case enter into the kingdom of heaven.' (Matt. 5:20)

Is that justice? According to that statement, then, the criterion is not whether a person lives a lawful and orderly life, but solely whether or not he is agreeable in the eyes of God, or the gods. A roulette game of grace, as it is still played in Lourdes today: one person is healed, the other is not.

At the same time, Jesus announces that all who 'are persecuted for righteousness' sake' would be blessed. (Matt. 5:10) How so? For the sake of which righteousness?

Contradiction after contradiction—explainable in that they are, after all, not utterances of the historic Jewish folk hero Jesus, but keep-up-the-good-fight slogans of the gods; for it would appear that the gods, finding themselves in a tight corner, were confusedly making threats and promises for all they were worth, just as, approximately two thousand years later, one Dr Joseph Goebbels did before the 'final victory'. In both cases the end came soon after the pronouncement.

At some time between 12,000 and 8000 BC there began the final and conclusive war between gods and Titans, or between the Aesir and the giants, as described in the Edda. [28]

This fight was not for the Earth, but for the entire solar system in which both sides appear to have had bases. The surface of 'Mahar', the heavenly body closest to the Earth (presumably the moon, which in those days was considered both lovely and habitable), is burnt to ashes through the 'beam from Shiva's third eye' (the Indian *Matsyapurana* 1:11 to 2:20); smaller celestial bodies (steered by artificial means?) crash onto the Earth ('And the stars of heaven fell unto the earth . . .' (Rev. 6:13)); continents sink; tidal waves race around the globe, and only a few human beings escape on mountaintops and in 'arks'—the '*Götterdämmerung*' has begun.

Today, when it is considered feasible to dislodge the smaller of the two Martian moons from its course by means of atomic explosions, and while American laser weapons are already in a position to set any object at a distance of several miles on fire—today it is surely no longer possible to dismiss these matters as figments of the imagination.

42

Besides, even atlantologists such as Otto H. Muck[29] assert that around the year 8498 BC a planetoid plunged into the ocean near the Bahamas, triggering enormous geological catastrophes.

In his book *Enträtselte Vorzeit*, Karl F. Kohlenberg has authoritatively reconstructed and described the fierceness of the final struggle of the gods, and its consequences.

But ultimately—whether decades or centuries later—the struggle ended and the curtain came down on the greatest cosmic drama of all times. Gone are the Titans, Asurs and giants, as are most of the gods; the few that survived gradually merged with what was left of the human race, and in the course of further millenia became legendary figures and, ultimately, gods.

'But ask you after giants, you'll find them never more . . .', reads a poem of the German Romantic period.

The question is repeatedly asked: Why has nothing, not the slightest trace, ever been discovered of these gods who in all probability lived and walked in the flesh on our planet—not even a screw from one of their machines or perhaps a simple trouser button?

Well, it would be almost a miracle if we did find something, for one point must be borne in mind: These gods or occupying forces from space were presumably small in number, at the most a few hundred or a few thousand. They seemed to be scattered everywhere and were known by different names all over the world; thus, thanks to the technical means at their disposal, they were able to control the entire Earth with their small detachment.

Their bases were small and not as magnificent as those man-made imitation temples and castles; they were no bigger than the small American and Russian bases in the Arctic and Antarctic. If a major disaster were to occur there, no trace of them might ever be found.

Besides, it may be assumed that during the course of the war against the Titans, the gods' bases and installations were either evacuated or destroyed, the latter by enemy action or natural disaster. We must always draw the analogy with modern warfare: as long as the communications of a threatened fortress or position keep functioning, everything movable can be removed by air and the rest blown up. All that is left behind are ruins and possibly a few soldiers who missed the last plane.

And that is how weakened those gods who were left behind must have been, after the last spaceship had lifted off from a tortured Earth, and after the last energy transmitter station had been put out of action. For a time, perhaps, they were able to fool the people with the help of their remaining arms and machines, but that, too, must have come to an end. Either they were killed, or graciously taken into the community. In the year 500 BC the Greek poet Pindar remarked almost scornfully:

> 'Of the same lineage are men and gods,
> And both draw breath through one mother. . . .'

At present, the 'white masters' of former times fare no better in Africa and other developing areas. Perhaps, even in a hundred years' time, people will look for their traces in vain—why should it have been any different for the gods whose presence goes back ten thousand years or more?

Jungles, oceans and shifting sand have swallowed their few remains. To find them would be harder than finding the celebrated needle in the haystack. Remember that it was only a few years ago that whole cultures and cities, like those of the Hittites in the Near East, as well as still completely unexplored fields of ruins in Afghanistan, were found. It is therefore likely that, as far as concrete facts are concerned, we shall have to rely on indirect references (which, nonetheless, need not be any the less convincing).

The well known German prehistoric scholar Leo Frobenius,[30] for instance, has been unable to determine why there should have been so many mines in parts of Africa in prehistoric times; for this large number cannot be justified by the requirements of the people living there at that time, even if one were to suppose that there had been a flourishing export trade. For whom were these large quantities of ore mined?

Puzzling, too, is the technique of processing ore, surprisingly well perfected in some parts of the world, while elsewhere Stone Age methods prevailed. There is some kind of industrial site, dating back to about 3000 BC or even earlier, which was exposed during excavations in the city of Uruk in Mesopotamia. There were metal foundries and installations for smelting at extremely high temperatures; there were iron ploughs to which a sort of sowing machine with a funnel was attached;[31] Korium Megertchian, a member of the Armenian Geological Institute, unearthed a similar industrial town at Medzamor in Armenia, where, according to tradition, the workers carried out their tasks with gloves and protective masks, similar to those used today—and that was 5000 years ago.

With normal evolution, such techniques would take thousands of years to develop. However, at Uruk and Medzamor they did not. These cities and cultures appear almost overnight, as if produced from a hat. Could it really have happened like that? And if it did, who was responsible?

What is characteristic and tragic about these very advanced early civilizations that were way ahead of later periods (at present the invention of the iron plough has been placed in the La-Tène period (from about 500 BC), to say nothing of the sowing machine) is that they cropped up only individually all over the world. Like rockets, they flared up only to die out again just as suddenly and to sink back into ignorance and primitiveness.

This may be interpreted thus: In these cases, individual 'divine development assistants' were at work, like the Thot of the Egyptians (the Greeks had Hermes), who is supposed to have taught them arithmetic, writing, land surveying, astronomy, nursing and gymnastics.[32]

As history has shown (and is showing again in connection with latter-day development aid) the success of their activities was shortlived.

The underdeveloped countries of today are interested less in the culture and painstaking constructive work which is brought to them by idealistic emissaries from the West, and more in those things with whose help one may wield power. The situation was exactly the same in the days of our ancestors.

The helpers who were looking after development and order had gone away—the Greek historian Herodotus (5th century BC) writes of the Pelasgi, the earliest inhabitants of Greece: 'They gave them the name of "gods", that is to say "order-makers", because in all matters they produced order, distributing all gifts as they wished'.[33] No sooner had they gone than the people (or rather the rulers among them!) began to neglect their allotted share in skills useful for life here on Earth, such as making ploughs, ore processing, etc. These skills at best remained dormant; usually they were forgotten altogether. To men, half-roused by the gods from a million years of somnolence, it seemed much more important to emulate their masters, whom they hated and worshipped in turn, in their attitude to power and rulership. What was most impressive about them was their weapons, their ability to transform themselves, to seem immortal, to ascend to heaven.

To emulate them, and to copy their achievements, was the object of entire peoples and generations. This is how, while the rabble remained as primitive, ignorant and poor as ever, those awe-inspiring temples, pyramids and towers came to be built in Central and South America, in the Orient and in Asia—stone stereotypes of high-voltage plants, reactors, launching pads and energy transformers. They were mightier and more imposing than their technological originals, but completely ineffectual. Their practical use was reserved strictly for the benefit of the rulers, the priests and the kings: with these monuments, and with the dread of the gods programmed so deeply into their minds, domination and exploitation of the people were easy matters.

Nevertheless it would seem that during the period after their disappearance, Europe too shared this emulation of the gods. What one might almost term its advertising slogan was coined in the Brahmanic words: 'We must do what the gods did.'[34] Doing what the gods did was divine service and lethal fashion:

46

The gods' interplanetary traffic consisted of rocket-shaped vehicles. Once, according to tradition, one of the gods, Odin, was apparently wounded by a native lance before he could reach and start up his vehicle, and these rocket-shapes were thus regarded as sacred. In several tribes, such as the Semnones, it became customary for sons of royal ancestry to let themselves be hanged from a tree and pierced by a lance, convinced that they would be able to rise after a few days.[35] In this wretched manner hundreds died, but none rose again.

Because the gods allegedly 'sloughed their skin,' during their partial transformation it became the practice to flay people, voluntarily or by force. During human sacrifice ceremonies, Xipe Indian priests[36] slipped into the skin which they had removed from their living victims. 'With their skin I cover the pillar...', says the report of the Assyrian king Tiglatpileser of the 12th century BC,[37] referring to his enemies. Skin, after all, was considered to be something special.

At intervals during the period of their active work on Earth the gods, either when they were on leave or when their period of service had expired, apparently went to their spaceships or energy transport vehicles and vanished without trace. Men would copy them in this respect too: in ancient Mexico and elsewhere[38] thousands of voluntary and compulsory victims were taken to the temple pyramids, the 'farewell mountains', and there (since they could obviously not rise to heaven) they were killed, having previously been accorded every honour of a farewell to the gods. In some African tribes, like the Yorubas and the Dahomees,[39] their town rulers were poisoned after only two years' reign—altogether a negative solution which eliminated the best and most able of mankind: all in honour of the gods.

The gods were often identified by Earth dwellers with their machines and vehicles;[40] the divine 'bulls', for instance, seem to have been some kind of tank capable of flight and, for that reason, were often depicted as animal-human hybrids. At times the natives may have

*succeeded in 'killing' these god-beasts, whereupon their
fuel would flow out and would naturally be mistaken
for blood. All this is probably the origin of the
misconceptions concerning the mysterious qualities of
divine blood.*

There is an example of this that it will be hard to better: It is
said that one day the legendary smith Hephaestus[41] (a
Titan!) built an iron giant for King Minos of Crete by the
name of Talos whose task it was to protect the island from
invasion. This Talos had the head of a bull (!) and a single vein
which ran through his body and was closed with a bronze
plug.

Three times each day, so the legend goes, the iron giant
strode round the island and destroyed any foe who came into
view with his 'fiery glances' (today we might perhaps call
them laser beams). It is said that while he was doing this he
would grin horribly, and that he wore this ghastly grin when
repulsing the invading Sardinians (hence the expression 'a
sardonic smile').

It was the cunning Medea who finally managed to defeat
Talos by secretly removing the plug that kept his vein sealed:
Talos bled to death.

Here, then, we have the 'divine blood' in which the natives
may have rolled after a victory over a vehicle or a robot, as
Siegfried rolled in the dragon's blood (probably another
robot fighting machine); this was to obtain both its power
and its invulnerability, and possibly they drank it too (as
several of the conquerors of 1945 drank eau-de-cologne):
fuel, petrol.

Tales of such struggles with the gods' vehicles were handed
down and recorded from generation to generation: 'My dear
friend, we have defeated the divine beast; may we not now
say that we shall be renowned among our descendants?' reads
the Sumerian Gilgamesh epic which was scratched on clay
tablets in about 1700 BC; however, it may go back to much
older Hurrithic legends.[42] This passage is the hero Gilgamesh
addressing his friend Enkidu, after they had together killed a
'bull' which had come 'from out of the sky' and which was

said to have killed 800 people.

Presumably the pilots and passengers of captured and destroyed divine vehicles were killed too, and occasionally devoured: by eating the gods it was hoped (possibly in vague recollection of the gods' cell-transplant methods) to obtain an increase of physical and mental powers. With that cruel consistency of which only men are capable, the human representatives of the gods were themselves later killed, eaten and their blood drunk.

This is clearly expressed in Revelation 19:17-18: 'And I saw an angel standing in the sun; and he cried with a loud voice saying . . . That ye may eat the flesh of kings, and the flesh of captains and the flesh of mighty men . . .'.

It was perhaps from this tradition and not only from lack of animal protein that cannibalism took its roots, roots which flourished even where there was an adequate supply of game and meat—e.g. in Britain and Europe. Here cannibalism did not appear before the Neolithic Age (between approximately 6000 and 2000 BC)—that is to say when the gods, from whom in the last analysis it originates, had already been and gone again.[43]

In Britain it was customary for a long time[44] to eat the brains of dead chiefs and of one's own parents, while in the Hungarian Bükk mountains a place was discovered where at least twenty-five people had found their way into other people's stomachs.[45]

Doubtless there was genuine cannibalism too, especially in times of want, but first and foremost it was more likely to have been a hallowed ritual, a theory strengthened by what was frequently a most careful and most affectionate burial of the bones of those who had been sacrificed.

Solomon too complains about this holy/unholy cannibalism when he speaks of his countrymen, 'devourers of men's flesh and the feasts of blood.' (Wisd. 12:5)

Presumably Solomon would have been surprised had he heard what Jesus is reputed to have said later in the synagogue of Capernaum: 'Whoso eateth my flesh, and drinketh my blood, hath eternal life.' (John 6:54)

This statement is repeated emphatically several times: 'He

that eateth me, even he shall live by me.' (John 6:56-7) There is no trace here of a simply more-or-less external identification of bread and wine with flesh and blood, as with the later Last Supper. It is no more than an offer of self-sacrifice for the purpose of consumption as a religious rite. The words which the gospel-writer John puts in the mouth of Jehoshua have only the most tenuous connection with Jewish Passover rites or with the rites of the sect of the Essenes, of which Jesus is said to have been a member. They are the words of a demigod or king of much earlier times, who in piously dutiful imitation of the gods had to allow himself to be killed and eaten.

Although, as already mentioned, that rite was based on a terrible error, it was nevertheless an honourable duty; and if a sufficient number of volunteers could not be found, they forced people to do it, like prisoners of war. Indeed, for many thousands of years people have spilled the blood of others in the name and in imitation of the gods.

In his book *Der gehenkte Gott* Erich Zehren remarks on this particularly sad chapter in the inglorious history of mankind: 'Wherever the clear gaze of Helios rested, he would see the sons of kings of divine ancestry hanging from trees, pierced by lances, dismembered and burnt. The names of these young men, led to the sacrifice and then sacrificed, may be unknown, but in many a province there are not enough forests, were one to see them all hang together, they who died on earth for the glory of heaven.'

This part-sadistic, part-masochistic craving for blood has its sequel in Christianity: the martyrs (whose number is often exaggerated and unequal to that of men, women and children who were later killed by Christians in the name of God) appeared to want nothing more than to perish on the sand of the arena. Often they consciously provoked it since they could thus even in a small way emulate their saviour, who had allegedly allowed himself to be killed as *agnus dei* ('Lamb of God'); they consumed his 'body' and his 'blood', albeit symbolically, but basically no differently from the way in which their forefathers consumed the real flesh and blood of their gods and their kings.

In all probability a modern Christian would be most indignant if one were to tell him that the core of his belief—the *communio*, in which he is linked with the deity by consuming it—points either to age-old cannibalistic rites or to quite realistic events such as the destruction of the technical appliances of the gods.

> *But any unselfconscious visitor from space arriving on Earth today would surely fail to understand why large sections of mankind worship their god by eating and drinking him.*

It is a fact, at any rate, that all the features of the Christ legend connected with this tradition—the hanging from the stake, the piercing with the lance, as well as the sepulchre, resurrection and ascension—were known thousands of years before the birth of Jesus. The figure of *Chrêstòs* (the Anointed) as the one who would fulfil that heritage of the gods was preprogrammed and prefabricated down to the last detail, and all Jesus really had to do was to carry out 'what had been written'. His later authors let him say so quite unequivocally: 'Think not that I am come to destroy the law, or the prophets: I am not come to destroy, but to fulfil. . .'. (Matt. 5:17)

It is likely that the Jewish-Essene evangelist Jesus of Nazareth himself had no idea at all of the reality and tradition of the gods, as most recent research has shown: [46,47] he did not regard himself as their successor, but rather as the earthly Messiah expected by the prophets who would re-establish the earthly kingdom of the Jews. And it was probably for that, and not for some nebulous 'kingdom of heaven', that he let himself be nailed to the cross; it was Paul and other later authors of the New Testament who pressed him into the precast mould of a god, or the son of a god.

Jesus the man was not to blame, for he knew nothing about it. But those who later gave him a completely different personality knew better, and one therefore might apply to at least some of them (especially to Paul) the modified Bible phrase: 'Lord, do not forgive them, for they knew what (falsehoods) they were writing!'

51

3 Born of a virgin

There are two factors which have been of far-reaching significance in the spread of the Christian faith all over the world: the apostle Paul and the belief in the Queen of Heaven, the Virgin Mary.

Without Paul there could have been no Christian religion and no Church. History's first publicity manager, it was he alone who built up the scarcely-known miracle rabbi Jeshu in the same way that stars of all kinds are managed and built up today. As is usually the case in such situations, he started with little to go on, for as far as the historic figure of Jesus of Nazareth is concerned, all that many can say after decades of critical research is that he lived some time around the year zero of our reckoning; and that he was a Jewish itinerant preacher who was executed for his opposition to the executive power.[1] Paul did not know much more as he had never met Jesus in person.

The life, work and death of Jesus (or Joshua, Jehoshuah or Jeshu) were neither exceptional nor peculiar. At that time there was continual unrest and revolt in the Roman-occupied kingdom of the Jews, as well as hundreds of executions. After Herod's death there was no lack of adventurers wanting to usurp the role of King of the Jews. Thus, to quote an example, Simon, one of Herod's servants, had placed the crown on his own head and roamed the country with a gang of robbers;[2] likewise a shepherd called Athronges and his gang blackmailed and murdered Romans and Jews loyal to the King, and on one occasion even cut an entire Roman cohort to pieces. 'Many of the noblest men were murdered, allegedly for liberty's sake, but in reality from lust for booty . . .', complained Josephus. The Romans reacted vigorously and in the only way to be expected from an occupying force: their governor Quintilius Varus, a predecessor of Pontius Pilate, suppressed an incipient revolt with the help of his legionaries and Arab auxiliaries and had two thousand suspected Jews nailed to the cross.

It is understandable, then, that after the arrest of the alleged conspirator Jesus, the majority of Jews might have considered it more sensible that this one man should die than possibly thousands later on.

'Ye know nothing at all, Nor consider that it is expedient for us, that one man should die for the people, and that the whole nation perish not,' High Priest Caiaphas (John 11:49-50) implores the High Council, and he wins acceptance for his realistic view.

It was not unfounded hatred against Jesus which led to the Jews demanding his death, but the fear of punitive sanctions by the occupying power, should he foment another revolt. For Pontius Pilate the Jesus case was certainly one of many. Whether the self-appointed rabbi called himself King of the Jews or not was a matter of indifference to him, but Jesus was alleged to have called for a tax strike too, and that was rebellion. On top of that the accused remained stubbornly silent and 'answered him to never a word' (Matt. 27:12-14) which, according to Roman law, was tantamount to a confession. In any case it seemed that this strange 'hippie' was actually asking to be put on the cross.

And put on the cross he was, whereupon the matter seemed to have ended. Historians and statesmen of the first two centuries after Christ took no notice of him as a historic personality, only of the religious movement which had started after his death.

'On account of some dead man called Jesus of whom Paul has asserted that he is alive': that is all the Roman Governor Festus knew of Jesus when, about thirty years after his death, he was asked to judge the apparently somewhat disturbed Paul.[3] (Acts 25:19)

It is likely that not much more than remarks of that nature would have remained of the sect of the 'Nazarenes', as they called themselves, had it not been for this man by the name of Saulus, or Saul (in Hebrew: Shaul; as a Roman citizen he always bore his Hellenistic name of Paulus, and thus did not adopt it at a later date!). On behalf of the ruling party of the Pharisees he fanatically persecuted the Nazarenes, and (if credence may be given to the research results of present-day historians) was an epileptic. During a fit which occurred while he was on a journey to Damascus, the twenty-five-year-old Paul thought he saw 'a light from heaven' and heard the voice of Jesus, whom he never knew personally (Acts 9:3-6). Result: Paulus/Shaul, the blind-with-rage 'Gestapo-man', defected to the enemy, and turned from being a fanatical persecutor into a fanatical champion of this new doctrine which, in those days, had not yet amounted to a doctrine.

The first Christians were nothing but a motley crowd of disgruntled Jews, slaves and proletarians who had heard talk of a saviour and to whom they looked for an improvement of their earthly lot and for some kind of world revolution, in the same way as the followers of other sects and secret societies. Paul then offered them his services as minister of progaganda, as it were. Indeed, he seems to have been some kind of Joseph Goebbels of the past; he was short, with bulging eyes, and ugly,[4] but tough and obsessed with his idea.

The procurator Festus could not dissuade him when (with the best intentions—for, after all, Paul was a Roman citizen) he shouted at him: 'Paul, thou art beside thyself, much learning doth make thee mad!' (Acts 26:24)

With unequalled enthusiasm and zeal—'. . . I laboured more abundantly than they all' he says of himself in 1 Corinthians 15:10—Paul created for the executed Jesus (of whose resurrection there were either no reports at all or only vague rumours) the 'image' of the truly risen and only Son of God and Redeemer. To do this he drew heavily, unscrupulously and with abandon on every myth and legend about the gods known to him as an educated man.

54

He was now armed with this identikit picture of Jesus, the man with the 'giant healing power'. It was so distorted and twisted a picture that it led to frequent quarrels between Paul, the early Christians, and his fellow apostle Peter.[5] He travelled through many countries. On four of his mission-journeys he travelled no less than 8000 miles, proffering his Christ story everywhere. Sometimes he was successful, at other times not. In Ephesus he was shouted down by the crowd who were infuriated by his provocations, chanting for hours on end, 'Great is Diana of the Ephesians!' (Acts 19:34); in Athens he was laughed at and chased out of town—they had heard similar stories about the gods before and knew them well enough for what they were.

But Paul was stubbornly undaunted, for the competition of other Christs (= 'Anointed') and redeemers of mankind was too fierce. There was, for example, one Apollonius of Tyana, from the Near Eastern province of Cappadocia, who had travelled around the country at about the same time as Jesus, preaching chastity and the turning away from blood sacrifices; who had performed miracle cures and raised people from the dead; and who was also worshipped as the Son of God. In many places temples had been erected to him and coins struck in his memory, which was still honoured by the emperors Caracalla, Aurelian and Alexander Severus.[6,7] He is said to have been incarcerated in Rome and to have died, almost a centenarian, at Ephesus, whereupon he appeared once more to his followers and subsequently ascended bodily into heaven.

Moreover there were many places where for more than two hundred years there had been the temples of the Egyptian god Serapis who, like the legendary Greek physician Aesculapius (and like Christ), is said to have effected miracle cures and raised the dead—Aesculapius was credited with six![8,9]

Such was the competition. But, at the same time, such was the material which Paul used in the fashioning of his Christ figure.

There is one difference, though, between the numerous other 'Eleuthérioi' (= Redeemers) and Jesus of Nazareth: they did not have the good fortune of possessing a clever publicity manager like Paul. But for that, who knows, today people might have been praying to Apollonius of Tyana.

In fairness, though, one must recognize that the genuine and real Jesus could not have anticipated his posthumous publicity.

For his part, Paul could be satisfied when in the year of grace 67, under the Emperor Nero, he was executed at Rome: his 'Myth of the First Century' had caught on, just as, 1866 years later, the 'Myth of the Twentieth Century' of the National Socialist party ideologist Alfred Rosenberg caught on; like the latter, it eventually became the only officially recognized and privileged ideology. True, it has lasted somewhat longer. The other authors of the first Jesus wave, the evangelists Mark, Matthew, Luke and John (not one of whom was an eye-witness in the passion and death of their saviour), did not enter the market until decades later; and their first-hand accounts (which in turn have been preserved only in second- or third-hand copies) bear eloquent witness to that fact.

Diligent students of the Bible have worked out that there are between 50,000 and 100,000 differences in the various gospel manuscripts.[10,11,12] As early as AD 370, Hieronymus complained about this when he intended translating these fragments into Latin on behalf of Pope Damasus. He wrote to the Pope that it was a dangerous presumption to try to compose a Bible containing the correct text, for there were marked variations between all extant copies of the (not extant) original text.

There would therefore appear to be not one single authentic text in the Bible, and the most essential statements of Christian doctrine thus originate from Paul.

It is Paul, and not Peter, who is the 'rock' on which Christianity is founded, and judging by his share in its form and content, it ought rightly to be called 'Paulinity'; of the Jewish rabbi Jehoshua there are only trace elements left in it.

The rest are the adopted (not to say stolen) ideas of ancient mythology of the gods and thus, in the last analysis, the tradition of the human astronaut-gods themselves.

In this sense, to the earlier statement 'No Christianity

without Paul' would have to be added '. . . and no Christ, no Paul and no Christianity without the "gods".' Without their technical miracles and without their ascensions, the subsequent alleged miracles and resurrection of Jesus of Nazareth would not have been possible.

But, we may ask, did not Paul, notwithstanding his perfection as a religion-maker, disregard one factor which later contributed, perhaps more than his 'Jesus Christ—Superstar', towards the almost epidemic way in which Christianity spread all over the world? (It has 924 million believers, or 26·5 per cent of the world population; it tops the list, leading Islam with its 14 per cent.) He did indeed—and his 'X-factor' is the female element. It was only its inclusion which gave Christianity an advantage over such purely 'male' religions as Judaism, Parseeism and Islam.

Only god *and* goddess make the picture complete.

Our otherwise so clever Paul *ought* to have seen this from the example of existing cults, but he was, after all, a confirmed (or conditioned by his former faith) woman-hater: 'Let your women keep silence in the churches'; 'Wives, submit yourselves unto your own husbands, as unto the Lord'; 'But I suffer not a woman to teach. . .'. (1 Cor. 14:34; Eph. 5:22; 1 Tim. 2:12) He did not *want* to know anything about it, or about the incipient gossip of his Lord and Saviour's virgin birth which later became the dogma and foundation of Catholicism.

Of course, his story was no more new and original than most of the other stage properties of the Pauline Messiah story; virgin conception and virgin birth originate from models which are thousands of years old, and thus from the gods; and any 'son of god' of that era *had* to be of divine-virgin birth. His public expected it of him, just as today they expect film stars and top sportsmen and women to be and to remain unmarried.

The virgin birth of Jesus was a concession to non-Jewish Christian party candidates and to old myths of the gods. The Jews, though, always inclined towards gossip and mockery, took a different view: they asserted that Miriam (=Mary) had been thrown out by her husband Joseph because she had had an affair with Pandera, a Calabrian captain in the occupying army and whose child was Jesus.[13]

Perhaps this might explain Christ's strange aversion to his mother ('Woman, what have I to do with thee', John 2:4), which finds expression even on the cross when he addresses her almost cynically: 'Woman, behold they son!' (by which he refers to John—John 19:26). The mother-son relationship seems to have been an uneasy one on both sides, for Luke (2:48) lets Mary violently reproach the youthful Jesus who had run off to the temple: 'Son, why hast thou thus dealt with us', and emphasizes the fact that she kept Jesus' pert reply 'How is it that ye sought me? (Luke 2:42) 'in her heart' (Luke 2:51).

On the other hand, the name of the supposed father Pandera (or 'Pantheras') leads directly to the Greek goddess Athena Parthenos (=Athena the Virgin) and thus to the mythical context.

But then perhaps both assertions are correct: Jesus was an illegitimate child (Luke 3:23: '. . . being (as was supposed) the son of Joseph . . .') and was later linked with the traditional virgin birth.

The tradition of virgin mothers is as old as the hills, while in this context one must distinguish between two categories: (a) mortal women who, after association with a god or gods and generally after 'annunciation' by an 'angel' (=messenger), gave birth to a child; and (b) goddesses who gave birth parthogenetically (virginally). In this connection, particularly in the second case, there is the question of whether this was really always the case (in itself, artificial impregnation is no problem and true virgin conception is medically and biologically quite feasible) or whether with this claim the divine ladies in question merely wished to hush up an 'accident' in their sex lives.

About a thousand years before an angel is supposed to have appeared to the wife of the village carpenter Joseph announcing the birth of the future Messiah, the wife of Manoah the Danite received a similar visit from a messenger of the Lord. He announced to the barren woman the birth of a 'Nazarite unto God': 'Behold now, thou *art* barren, and bearest not: but thou shalt conceive and bear a son. . . .'. 'And the woman bare a son, and called his name Samson: and the child grew, and the LORD blessed him.' (Judg. 13: 2-25)

It is that same Samson who, according to the Old Testament, became the liberator of his people Israel after forty years of Philistine rule. The story of the miraculous fertilization of Manoah's wife contains other very strange details: The angel came once again 'unto the woman as she sat in the field' (Judg. 13:9); she called her husband who spoke to this strange messenger: '*Art* thou the *man* [author's italics] that spakest unto the woman?' (Judg. 13:11) The messenger confirmed this and proceeded to give the woman instructions for her pregnancy: 'She may not eat of any *thing* that cometh of the vine, neither let her drink wine or strong drink, nor eat any unclean *thing* . . .'. (Judg. 13:14)

Manoah wanted to kill a kid for the stranger, but the stranger said: 'Though thou detain me, I will not eat of thy bread.' (Judg. 13:16)

Manoah asked the man's name, but he gave an evasive reply: 'Why askest thou thus after my name, seeing it is secret?' (Judg. 13:18)

But in the end Manoah did sacrifice a kid, and the 'angel of the Lord', having previously done 'wondrously' (what it was that he did wondrously is not revealed), 'ascended in the flame'. 'And Manoah and his wife . . . fell on their faces to the ground.' (Judg. 13:20) The angel 'did no more appear'— only the child was there.

Translated into modern and matter-of-fact language, this same story would read something like this : It would appear that gods holding subordinate rank (precisely those 'messengers') were amusing themselves on Earth, posing as emissaries of the Lord, sleeping with the wives of the mortals and vanishing without revealing name or rank—a tradition among soldiers of all times. At best they left behind (as in the case of Manoah's wife) advice in case of pregnancy before departing 'in the flame' in some vehicle.

Left behind were the earthmen and their impregnated wives, and to cap it all, they regarded the whole event as miracle and grace.

Of course, any children fathered in this way were superior to all others; they were—were they not?—children of the gods, though not begotten by a Holy Ghost but rather by very much alive human beings.

The story of Manoah and his wife captivates us above all by its sober clearness: the woman who, with honest ingenuousness, relates her nocturnal adventure with the angel to her husband; she sees him (he seems to have had something like pangs of conscience) again in the field; he gives her hints for her pregnancy; she calls her husband; he speaks, quite normally, to the stranger (and by no means to a ghost or an apparition); and later she does in fact give birth to an unusual child. One may assume that events of that kind did not take place only 3000 years ago, for by that time there would hardly have been any gods left on Earth, but already much earlier. But because men thought them sensational, they were handed down by word of mouth and incorporated in the respective myths, as in the Manoah-Samson case and ultimately also in the Jesus-Mary legend, which in this respect is practically a word-for-word copy. It is certain that no angel appeared to Joseph's wife Miriam, simply because there were no such beings.

> *Considered from this angle, the whole story of 'Jesus, Son of God' is nothing but the last yellowed copy of a film which was shot umpteen thousand years ago.*

People to whom such statements seem irreverent may care to remember that the mothership of Mary was 'decided' upon at the Council of Ephesus in AD 431 and fiercely resisted by the Nestorians who were prepared to see Jesus and Mary as simple human beings.

The earliest known mention of a virgin birth by a mortal woman occurs, incidentally, in the epic of Gilgamesh,[14] where it is written that the daughter of King Enmekar of Uruk, although locked up in a tower by her father, had, 'as determined by the gods', born a son: the hero Gilgamesh.

However, we have already seen that it was not only mortal women who gave birth virginally, but also goddesses, who were the female crew members of the colonizers from space. Here it appears to have been not always an excuse for an indiscretion, but actual parthogenic practices or artificial insemination.

In a text from the time of the Egyptian New Empire (1580 to 1080 BC) the (originally Ugarithic and Babylonian) goddesses Anath and Astarte are described as 'the great goddesses who do not conceive, but give birth'.[15] Similar claims were made for Hera, the official spouse of Zeus. After the birth of Hera's daughter Athena, Ares says to her: 'Yourself you bore the destructive daughter. . .' (Homer, *Iliad*), while Chrysippus[16] writes: 'With the aid of art [techné] she bore her son Hephaestus without aegis-shaking Zeus.' Was Hera so ugly or was Zeus so impotent? In view of his innumerable *amours* with mortal women, that is not very likely. What then really did happen?

This whole affair, only faint echoes of which are to be found in Greek legends of the gods, can be considered quite realistically and simply: the gods which had come to Earth from the cosmos were few in number. They were predominantly male, but there were a few women as well. They had their own laws which, following the principle of self-preservation, prohibited mingling with the natives. But mingle they did all the same. First, of course, were the men, and they were so thorough that their sexual achievements live on in legends and cults, as in the cult of Chons (or Hamutef), tutelary god of Thebes in Egypt, who was known as 'Master of the Maidens' and 'the god who abducts women'.[17]

At first the ladies followed their example a little more hesitantly (except where they confined themselves to self-fertilization, thus remaining within the law), but later on they proved no less energetic.

Greek mythology (one might call it pornography) says that Eos, the rosy-fingered goddess of dawn, although married to the Titan (!) Astraeus, had seduced several mortal men and carried them off to distant stars—a proper Messalina of ancient times.[18,19] Ganymede, one of her mortal paramours, is said to have been so fair that he found favour with Zeus himself and was appointed cup-bearer to the gods. The Masai in Africa recount[20] that a goddess called Heiterogob had fallen in love with the mortal hero Kintu, even taking him with her up to heaven, where thanks to her help Kintu passed every test the gods gave him with flying colours. Despite warnings by the Lord of Heaven and his wife Heiterogob, Kintu did make one mistake: because he had forgotten something 'up there', he tried to return once more, and this cost him and the children he had had with the goddess their lives.

There are many such legends. Another one which ends in death is recorded by several tribes in the jungle of the Gran Chaco of Brazil. A beautiful goddess came to Earth from Venus (?) and fell in love with a poor and not very handsome mortal man. She attempted to take him with her to Venus, but he died of cold in space.[21]

It is the end of this story that is puzzling. Where did the Indians in the sun-seared Gran Chaco find out that it was deathly cold in space? Most of the love stories between goddesses and mortal men have a dramatically tragic ending.

While their male colleagues usually took the easy way out and unceremoniously left their mortal mistresses (at best they were fobbed off with a few gold coins, as was the Greek princess Danaë by Zeus), it would appear that from time to time the goddesses displayed genuine feelings, even though by our standards their mortal boyfriends were not much more than savages.

The most moving love story of this kind is that of Eos. A short while ago we associated her with the name of Messalina, but she obviously had another side to her: One of her last loves on this world was Tithonus, a son of King Laomedon of Troy. Eos asked Zeus to confer the gift of immortality on him, and her wish was granted. The pair lived happily, far away from Earth, 'in the east by the river of the world' (possibly the Milky Way). But Eos had forgotten one thing: to demand, together with immortality, eternal youth for Tithonus. He aged, while she remained young; he grew more and more wrinkled and ever smaller, while Eos nursed him lovingly, until at long last he turned into a tiny insect with a shrill voice: the cicada.[22]

To resemble the gods even in part has never been accepted by mankind, and it was these hybrid children, begotten by gods or goddesses and mortals, who were made to feel the stigma of their birth: they were human as well as divine outcasts and as such they were frequently persecuted—by gods as well as men.

Horus, son of the Egyptian goddess Isis, was forced to change himself into a bull to escape from the persecution of the god Seth;[23] similarly Zeus was hidden from his own father Kronos on Crete by his mother Rea; and the above-mentioned Danaë had to hide her son Perseus, fathered by Zeus (?), from his grandfather Acrisius, who had been told by the Delphic Oracle that his grandson would be the cause of his death. The Oracle was right—during a sports competition Perseus inflicted a never-healing wound on his grand-grandfather's leg with a discus. To begin with, though, Acrisius had his daughter and her brat locked in a box and thrown into the sea (a first reference to the rush basket in which Moses was found), but luckily she was saved by fishermen.

A similar fate fell to Antiope, daughter of King Nycteus of Thebes and her twin sons Amphion and Zethus (also fathered by Zeus). In dread of her father she had to leave them behind to be looked after by shepherds in a remote district.

The fate of the bastard children of the gods may be glimpsed in legend and tradition. Sargon I, founder of the Accadian Empire (3000 BC), is said to have been found in a small bamboo box floating on the river Euphrates,[24] while Chandragupta, founder of the Hindu Maurya dynasty in 400 BC, was discovered in a jar on the threshold of a cowshed.[25] It is logical to presume that these special characteristics of divine origin—persecution and concealment—were transferred to and projected onto the Messiah/Jesus. The Holy Family, as it says in the New Testament, had to flee to Egypt from Herod's slaughter of innocent children. This is incorrect: King Herod never gave orders for the wholesale murder of children; Josephus Flavius, who is usually absolutely precise and does not spare Herod with his criticism, does not mention it.[26] Herod did have three of his own sons executed, but only after a proper trial, confirmed by the Roman Emperor Augustus, and then only because they had attempted to remove their aged and seriously ill father by poisoning him (he is thought to have suffered from cancer of the liver).

Thus the 'flight' of Joseph and Mary turns out to be a simple pretext that the as yet unborn Jesus might be said to have come 'from Egypt', from where Moses and his ancestors had come before him.

Finally this child of the Holy Ghost is born in a stable at Bethlehem, among shepherds and cattle. We have already seen some of the stage properties in the myths of Greek and Indian demigods. It may sound well round rural Christmas mangers, but it scarcely corresponds to historical truth. It is not certain where Jesus was born. What might be true is that the authors of the Messiah legends, from Paul to the later gospel writers, chose Bethlehem as the birth-place because:

> *There was an ancient place of worship in Bethlehem and a sacred grotto of the Babylonian-Syrian god of resurrection, Tammuz/Adonis; also Bethlehem was the city of King David (c. 1000 BC) from whose tribe, according to ancient Jewish belief, the long-awaited Messiah and liberator of the people would come.*[27]

Furthermore, we may note that the Three Kings, hurrying to Bethlehem, are stock components of many traditions (they are said to have come to Nero in the same way as they came to Herod). And Heracles, hero of ancient Greek legend, after much suffering and before being taken up to heaven by Zeus, concluded his earthly existence with the words: 'Father, I come—*it is finished!*'[28] These are the identical words used thousands of years later by Christ. We can therefore draw the conclusion that for his later biographers the real rabbi Jeshu merely served as a clothes-stand on which to hang the discarded wardrobes of former gods; or as a length of tape for the recording of texts which others had spoken.

At least Jesus died according to demigod tradition, albeit based on a misunderstanding—'in order to fulfil the law': on the cross. Other hybrid children of the gods did not fare so well; as unwelcome bastards they were frequently killed shortly after birth, sometimes by their real or imputed fathers, sometimes by their mothers. An example of this is found in the Nordic legend of Gudrun, who served up her own children roasted on a spit[29] to her husband. Hera too, without hesitation, flung her artificially conceived son Hephaestus down from heaven because he was so exceptionally ugly. Ever after that, so the story reads, Hephaestus limped. This same fact, by the way, has been claimed very persistently with regard to Jesus: he is said to have had a lame leg or foot;[30] this is unlikely, however, and is probably just another relic of the gods which had been taken over.

Religious child murders, though—and this is about the most horrible aspect of that pathological human craze for copying the gods—came to be the height of fashion for thousands of years; out of single cases of removing unwanted offspring grew a bloody ritual.

During excavations near a sacred stone of Astarte[31] hundreds of new-born babies' skeletons were found, while in the ruins of Carthage on the north African coast burnt offerings of babies were discovered buried in stone jugs—sacrificial offerings to the gods, as can be deduced from the inscriptions.[32]

The Mexican rain-god Tlaloc, too, was partial to sacrifices of children, whose tears were interpreted as raindrops. Both the Celts and the Slavs slaughtered children; and Solomon, in his 'Wisdom' (14:23), frets: '. . . they slew their children in sacrifices'. Hosts of murdered children haunt mankind's cults. Even in the Greece of splendid temples and lofty spiritual culture, Artemis Triclara, the 'thrice-wise', was annually given a sacrifice of a boy and a girl.[34]

There appears to be no explanation for the iniquity of hundreds of thousands of mothers who, contrary to the instinct of preservation of the species, surrendered their children and allowed them to be murdered, other than that of obtuse imitation of individual examples among gods and goddesses and of people who butchered illegitimate half-caste children for the purpose of preserving 'racial purity' (or simply from envy).

> *Or could there be still another interpretation? True, it would be so horrific that one hardly dare mention it, although many traditions and customs point to it :gods, and above all goddesses, had demanded and used embryos and newly-born babies in order to maintain their own youth and beauty.*

Only at first glance does this sound absurd and impossible. We should remember that some of the best cosmetics are made from the placenta of women giving birth, and further that the famous cell therapy of Professor Niehans, which helped many a film star and politician to renewed youth and vigour, is based on injections of the cell tissue of unborn and freshly-killed calves.

> *We must ask what might have caused the gods at first to regard those anthropoids populating the planet Earth as anything other than cattle, and to use them. After all, as legend has it, they exterminated entire races whom they considered defective without batting an eyelid.*

The view that these 'divine ones' were superior to us in the sense of morality as we understand it is not substantiated; presumably, with a few exceptions, their morality was quite different.

It is precisely this morality which finds expression in the phenomenon of child sacrifices. There can be no excuse: they demanded the sacrifices clearly and unequivocally. In Exodus it says unmistakably: 'The firstborn of thy sons shalt thou give unto me!' (Exod. 22:29); similarly 'Jahve' (Exod. 34:19): 'All that openeth the matrix *is* mine . . .'. The prophets mourn: 'Moreover thou hast taken thy sons and thy daughters, whom thou hast borne unto me, and these hast thou sacrificed' (Ezek. 16:20); '. . . in their own gifts in that they caused to pass through *the fire* all that openeth the

66

womb, that I might make them desolate, to the end that they might know that I *am* the LORD' (Ezek.20:26); '. . . of that command whereby the infants were slain' (Wisd. 11:7); '. . . slaying the children in the valleys under the clifts of the rocks'. (Isa. 57:5)

The first-born belonged to the gods—because they were freshest and best.

In this way we can understand that, for instance, Tantalus, who often had learned discussions with the gods, served them up his own son.[35]

It is unlikely that he wanted to test their omniscience, as later adaptations of the legends asserted. He intended to do them a favour and ingratiate himself with them. That it did not get him anywhere was his bad luck. Perhaps not all the gods ate children like their ancestor Kronos; after all, not every woman today uses placenta cosmetics, nor does every man undergo a course of cell therapy using the tissue of freshly-killed calves.

Invariably it was the gods' negative aspects which have been preserved. In order to emulate the desires of some of them for fresh cells, organs and blood, large numbers of children were sacrificed even when there were no gods left on Earth; live Maya and Aztec prisoners of war had their hearts, livers and other organs torn out as sacrifices on the altars of the gods even when there were no longer any prehistoric Professor Barnards or Niehans to undertake the task of organ transplants or cell tissue injections.

Today it is hard to imagine that from the dawn of mankind to the times of the Greeks and Romans child sacrifices were natural and everyday events. Girls were usually killed as a matter of course immediately after birth,[36] while the sacrifice of male children was later replaced by the use of lambs.

At times this resulted in a shortage of female offspring, which was why, for example, after the conquest of Midian, the Jews sacrificed only 1 per 1000 of the 32,000 virgins they found, i.e. 32, leaving the others for breeding.

All this happened perhaps only because it was considered the done thing to imitate the gods in this respect. It would

67

appear that advertisements to the effect that a long life can be obtained from the cells of freshly killed babies have been effective at all times.

Thus Atreus killed the sons of his brother Thyestes so that his ageing father could eat them; thus queen Procne served her son grilled to Tereus for supper;[37] thus, when it would not rain in Mexico, Africa and elsewhere, they quickly slaughtered a few dozen children. The sacrificial stones and altars of history ran with the blood of children. Even in or near the temple at Jerusalem such butcheries appear to have been committed. 'For when they had slain their children to their idols, then they came the same day into my sanctuary to profane it. . .', scolds Ezekiel (23:39). Ritual murder, for which the Jews have been falsely blamed, was not the exception but the rule, an aping of an orgy of slaughter and murder without equal and which can be traced back to the gods.

Regrettably these are not simply cheap Dracula or vampire stories. They are horrific reality, as inextricably linked with the prehistory of the Christian religions as everything else which originated with and came from the gods.

It is impossible to keep separate the individual threads which were ultimately woven into the fabric of this religion—gods and goddesses, blood myths and death myths, virgin birth as well as the sacrifice and resurrection of the Son of God—and to consider them separately, for then they would no longer have either meaning or context.

New light falls on a number of other questions and problems if they are considered from the point of view of the gods. There is for instance a lively discussion today about which form of society was likely to have predominated originally: Patriarchy or matriarchy. The answer is probably quite straightforward—both existed (which is how they later found their way into myths and religions). Where men were in command at the few landing places of the gods, there, subsequently, men would rule and 'male' religions predominate; where female commanders were in charge, there women would rule.

Jahve or Jehovah, the Jews' 'district commissioner' and tribal god, was doubtless a mortal, and not a very endearing specimen of the human race either. He was angry and cruel; he tormented the Jews under his command, and if they did not obey him, he annihilated them. 'And there went out fire from the LORD, and devoured them' it says about the disobedient sons of Aaron (Lev. 10:2). The Old Testament is full of such tales. In these incidents, it is not just a few but hundreds or thousands of Jews who are burnt or killed by rays—atomic or laser weapons.

When Lord Jahve needed money, he would hire out his slaves as guest workers. This may be read word for word in Judges, where it has been recorded as clearly and succinctly as a newspaper report: '. . . and he sold them into the hand of Chushanrishathaim King of Mesopotamia' (Judg. 3:8), or 'And the LORD sold them into the hand of Jabin King of Canaan, that reigned in Hazor.' (4:2)

The wailings of the Jews ('And . . . the children of Israel cried unto the LORD' (3:9 and 4:3)) did them no good at all, for that same King Jabin, for instance, to whom they had been hired for twenty years (with Jahve presumably pocketing the money), 'had nine hundred chariots of iron' (4:3). Is there anyone who does not immediately think of tanks built under licence from the gods?

Jehovah, not to mince words, appears to have been a very unpleasant and brutal slavedriver, a half-crazed butcher and a mass-murderer, and if today Jews as well as Christians still regard him as 'the Lord Zebaoth', then that is their look-out.

Were the divine ladies any better? Yes and no. Consider Athena, virgin daughter born after artificial insemination of a maritally frustrated mother. She behaved exactly as was to be expected of such a virgin: she cosseted and favoured her darlings such as Heracles, or Erichthonius, son of her artificially procreated brother Hephaestus whom she made King of Athens, giving him such excellent driving lessons that Zeus later transferred him to the stars as 'Charioteer'.

It is this story of Erichthonius which may be interpreted to contain remarkable references to the practice and dangers of artificial insemination at the time of the gods: he is really an 'indirect' son of Athena. One day Hephaestus had a sudden lust for his 'artificial' sister Athena and tried to ravish her in

69

his smithy. He failed because of the virgin's resistance, and his seed fell on the ground. Athena modestly trod it into the dust and it was hatched out by the earth goddess Gaea—an indication, perhaps, of the use of an artificial uterus? The prematurely born child was put into an incubator (Athena locked it into a 'solid basket'!). It lived, though like some kind of Thalidomide child: Erichthonius had crippled, 'snake-like' feet. Athena had him trained as a driver so that those poor feet should not be seen.[38]

Could this possibly be regarded as a first source for those reports about the limping Jesus? Was the chariot of Erichthonius perhaps an invalid carriage? We do not know, but the assumption readily suggests itself.

Let us return to our virgin Athena. We have seen that she was chaste; in consequence she was regarded as the guardian of propriety and order, both of which virtues she had taught the people. She gave them the plough and taught them the art of weaving;[39] she was the first to be called 'worker' (Greek: ergànêe) and, in this respect, was a predecessor of the industrious Martha of the Gospel of St Luke (10:41).

But at the same time Athena was a ferocious warrior and, with the spear as her second attribute (the wise owl on her hand was the first), a 'terrible goddess' (*Odyssey* 7:40), a 'capturer' and 'devastator of cities' (Aristophanes) who, 'shining from afar', flies through the army of the Greeks, inciting them to 'hideous struggle in battle' (*Iliad*, 2:450). In the beleaguered city of Troy the seer Helenus, son of Priam, vainly invited his fellow citizens to submit to and worship this Joan of Arc of old, if only she were to take pity on the 'babbling babes' (*Iliad* 6:86f.); she seemed greatly superior in arms and equipment. The stupid Trojans did not know that Athena was also the builder of *Argo*, the legendary speedboat of the Argonauts. Ultimately they were defeated by technology after an attack with armoured troop carriers—the Trojan Horse.

The goddesses appear as contradictory and unbalanced as the gods when we examine their cults: virgins, mothers and teachers—destroyers, sex symbols and whores. It was the goddesses who invented and supervised the 'oldest profession in the world'. It began as divine service, as in Uruk and Babylon more than 4000 years ago, where every woman, high- or low-born, had to give herself to a stranger once in her lifetime, and sacrifice her earnings to the 'great Mother', the Ishtar-Venus.[40] (Herodotus I/129)

This custom spread rapidly throughout the ancient world, assuming somewhat more terrestrial forms in the process. At Corinth it was customary to 'consecrate' to the temple of Aphrodite girls and women who served as prostitutes. This was done in such a sophisticated and lucrative manner that it might cause modern counterparts to go green with envy: on the one hand the servants of Aphrodite were at the disposal of visitors to the temple for their physical gratification; on the other hand it was considered a mark of religious good breeding to let these very same 'servants' join in the prayer with every petition presented to the goddess—as many as the petitioner could afford.[41] (Strabo VIII/6:20) And since at times the temple of Aphrodite at Corinth boasted more than a thousand prostitutes, it is not hard to imagine how rich it was.

It went without saying that at the great annual festivals of the whore-goddesses Aphrodite, Urania, Astarte, Cybele etc., there was complete sexual freedom among all the female participants.[42] Group sex seems to have had its origin here. But it would be a mistake to regard such cults and mysteries as mere pretext for sexual excesses; this may have been true later, and then only to a degree, but it was not the case originally.

The uncanny fascination which some of these goddesses must have exercised is illustrated by the thousands of young men who voluntarily castrated themselves before statues of, for example, Cybele and Atargatis in Asia Minor and Greece (this was compulsory for priests). They then exultantly flung their severed masculinity on the altars—a kind of veneration which would be unlikely to find many emulators today.

All these goddesses (or rather, the copies of much earlier human-astronaut originals preserved in their cults) are now dead and gone, with one exception: the Holy Virgin Mary, the only female figure to whom (within western civilization) divine honours are still accorded. It seems absurd and impossible to try to imagine any link between her and the bevy of ancient goddesses other than, at the outside, that of the virgin birth of her son. Such a link does exist, however, and it can be proved historically: not, of course, a link with the simple Jewess Miriam who gave birth to the mortal Jehoshuah, but with that artificially created figure of the same name who, in hundreds of legends and performances, displays herself as 'Mother of God' and 'Queen of Heaven'.

What applies to the traditional redeemer and god of ascension Jesus Christ applies also to her. Unfortunately the essential traits of her figure, too, are merely a tradition, inherited and taken over from the gods: of the human historic personality practically nothing is left.

There were, for instance, mothers of gods and queens of heaven long before the earthly existence of the mother of Jesus. In the Egypt of the third pre-Christian millenium it was the goddess Ma'at, or Hathor, and others who were revered as mistresses of heaven, while many pharaohs proudly claimed to be their sons.[43]   In the Holy Land itself, in Palestine, there was a goddess called Hepa who, in the middle of the second millenium BC, was regarded as just such a queen of heaven. Under the name of Hipa she was held to be the mother of Dionysus. And in the 11th century BC the Assyrian King Assurnasirpal prayed to the queen of heaven Ishtar, imploring her protection and confessing his sins.[44]

But the direct genealogical tree of the Christian queen of heaven leads to the ancient and eternally young Egyptian goddess Isis, spouse of Osiris and mother of the boy Horus—the Christ-child of the Egyptians.

The cult of Isis first flowered in the Middle Empire years (2263 – 2040 BC); but her rise to chief deity of the land of the Nile and mother of god—her statues show her sitting on her throne, suckling the child Horus—takes place only after the conquest of Egypt by the Persians (525 BC). Then began her victory march through the entire ancient world. In the 4th century BC the cult of Isis reached Greece, in the 3rd century Sicily and in the 2nd century Rome—the religion of a wife and mother who differs from the other goddesses, a

72

religion of the love of man.[45]

In Boeotia slaves were set free in the name of Isis and of her son Horus—two hundred years before Mary gave life to the redeemer of those who 'labour and are heavy laden' (Matt. 11:28). In the sanctuary of Eleusis near Athens a mystery play was performed annually in honour of the goddess in which her 'holy wedding' (*hieros gámos*), the virgin birth of the son of god and finally his ascension into heaven, were performed. 'Our mistress has borne a holy boy!' cried the enthusiastic spectators, who are said to have numbered tens of thousands. They began to sing, much as Christians do at Christmas.[46,47]

Isis was a goddess of peace and grace. Several times, so Livy and other Roman historians report, her priests saved cities from pillage and destruction solely by pointing out the existence of her sanctuary.

All the same, it took a long time before the Egyptian 'guest goddess' was officially recognized in Rome. In AD 19 Tiberius still ordered her sanctuaries to be destroyed and one of her priests to be crucified; but later Emperor Caligula built her a magnificent temple on the field of Mars, thereby granting her the right of citizenship. After only another forty years, the Emperor Domitian joined the procession and confessed himself a 'servant of Isis'.

To a worshipper of Christ and Mary, this cult would have seemed anything but strange. White-robed and tonsured priests walked at the head of the festive procession, followed by the Emperor and the dignitaries of the Empire. Then came the hymn-singing people, following the image of the mother of god, who was clad in long flowing robes of Hellenistic style and elaborately adorned with jewels and precious stones; all round the image burned hundreds of candles while incense wafted everywhere.[48]

It goes almost without saying that this Mother of God also possessed all the most popular attributes of other ancient goddesses: the moon at her feet, the stars round her head and the dove, ancient symbol of Ishtar, which in Christianity was to become the Holy Ghost.

The Roman rule of Isis lasted for a scant two hundred

years. In 313, after Christianity had been declared the official religion, the consul Nicomachus celebrated the last feast of Isis;[49] in 397 fanatical Christians destroyed her sanctuary at Alexandria, and everywhere else the temples of the 'heathen goddess' suffered the same fate.

The first Christians had no idea of the subsequent 'holiness' of their saviour's mother; not one of the apostles had mentioned this woman who was not particularly respected by her son; there was no Paul to promote her to a queen of heaven. Exceptionally, the revolution started from below, from the people, who had been accustomed to their virgin and mother goddess and who wanted to retain her.

It took a long time for the manipulators of the new faith to realize this. Only when they could not help noticing that their lambs, due to a naïve misunderstanding, still revered the images of the Isis-Mother with her Horus-Child,[50] did they grasp what was happening. At the Council of Ephesus (AD 413), in the face of much resistance from Christian 'Trotsky-ites', they forced the rank of Mother of God, which had belonged to Isis, onto Mary. That was an unequalled act of religious power politics, for there was even less information on the historic Mary than on her son Jesus, who had after all fulfilled at least *one* of the functions incumbent on a god by dying on the cross. Mary had done nothing like that. She had been only a humble wife and mother.

That this jiggery-pokery came off is no miracle. The cults and traditions of the goddesses were too deeply rooted in and beyond Rome, so deeply indeed that they were able to survive the transfer to Mary: basically it was enough to replace Isis with this historically so insignificant Mary—and nothing had changed at all, not in the myth, nor in her supposed history.

> It was a switching of names and actresses in the same play; Mary, the complete amateur, took over a leading role which in reality she could never have played—for she was, after all, no goddess.

Yet this was the Christian Church's greatest scoop: the
74

substitution of the 'extra', Mary, in place of the many familiar goddesses; the 'sweet virgin' Britomartis was as familiar to the Celts as the virginal Nerthus (Hertha), made pregnant by a god, to the ancient Germans.[51]

It was the same in Russia, South America and Africa—everywhere there were goddesses of this kind. This was quite logical, for in the last analysis they had been 'created' after identical archetypal divine models.

This was how Christianity was easily able to gain a foothold where there had previously been goddesses. All that was required was a new cast list; no new programme was needed.

Looked at from this angle, then, millions of Christians today worship not a Jewess called Miriam, who gave birth to a son called Jesus about 1974 years ago, but projections of some archaic goddesses; and they do so by using their old traditional names: Star of the Sea (*stella maris*), Gate of Heaven, Virgin Priestess (*virgo sacerdos*), Lodestar, Evening Star. (All these, note, are allusions to the cosmic relatedness of the old goddesses.)[52,53]

Nearly all the feast-days and holidays of Mary date back to other goddesses: May, the month of Mary, is the holy month of Artemis; 25 March (the Annunciation) corresponds to the Roman feast of Minerva; Mary's Assumption on 15 August to the Feast of Diana, etc.; while it is a matter of course that many of Our Lady's churches were built on or over the temples of her predecessors. This last gesture served to provide tangible evidence of the victory of Christianity over heathen goddesses. The Maria Antiqua at Rome stands in the place of the former temple of Juno; it was the same in the provinces of the Roman Empire.[54] This relief and replacement is also locally documented.

The same applies to the miracles imputed to Mary: goddesses have always 'appeared' to their followers, and just as there are allegedly 'weeping' pictures of the Madonna, two thousand years earlier Livy mentions (*Livius* 40:19) the weeping painting of the Roman goddess Juno.

Whatever one investigates in connection with Mary is,

on closer inspection, transformed into the essential characteristics and personalities of former (real) goddesses.

The humble Jewess Miriam presumably had as much trouble with her son Jesus as any of today's mothers whose offspring become hippies. But the figure people have turned her into is an artefact, a synthesis of the components of many other cults of goddesses (first and foremost, of course, of Isis), and anything which might be considered undesirable by the Church Fathers was carefully removed from it; for the old goddesses were not only good and noble; they were also human and had their faults as well as their virtues.

A final and obscure reminder of this is still to be found in the worshipping of the Black Madonna pictures, the most famous of which is at the Polish place of pilgrimage, Czestochawa.

The usual explanation is that the colours of the paintings have become oxidized or blackened by candle smoke. Perhaps so; but perhaps some of these paintings and icons have always been black, as it says in old texts of the Egyptian moon goddess: 'You are black and great. . .'.[55]

The Mother of God of the Church, though, must not be allowed to have such a blemish, but instead must be 'whiter than white', or else she would not (as Pope Pius XII announced on 1 November 1950) have gone bodily into heaven where now, according to a statement by the same Pope in 1943,[56] 'she rules together with her son'.

There is now only a minimal gap separating Mary from complete parity with the godhead. According to Christian doctrine Jesus ascended to heaven through his own power (and according to the technique of the astronauts); that is the 'ascensio'. According to the same doctrine, Mary was taken there by angels; that is the 'assumptio', her reception into heaven.

Even prior to the dogmatization of Mary's ascension, painters and sculptors gave her a pronouncedly divine characteristic: the 'mandala', an almond-shaped aura round the body which used to be the prerogative of Jesus

76

alone[57] and which is nothing but the pictorial representation of the physico-optical effects, as they might have appeared during the technological ascensions of the gods.

With Mary's reception into heaven the last link of a chain has been forged. Those very human ladies from another star, who landed on our planet in the dim and distant past, turned into goddesses and cults; they, in turn, produced the *one* new queen of heaven who (if only in the dogma of the Church and not in reality) has now returned to where her real ancestors had originated.

Thus the old order in heaven has been restored. As with the Egyptians' Isis and Osiris—sister and brother as well as man and wife—two godheads reside there once more, this time mother and son, Jesus and Mary.

The one who has stepped into the background is 'God the Father', the real lord of heaven; essentially his function is constitutional, like that of the monarchy in many countries today. Most of the divine functions have been taken over by Jesus: '. . . no man cometh unto the Father, but by me', is what Jesus said according to John (14:6). Miracles, good deeds and charity are Mary's department.

This is the true new Trinity, and no longer that of Father, Son and Holy Ghost.

Visits to virgins who are to bear gods are no longer necessary, and therefore no longer common. So the Holy Ghost, or *spiritus sanctus* (always a somewhat nebulous and unfathomable entity), has turned into a sort of Minister without Portfolio; into a word in creed and prayer, bearing no precise meaning; into a picture of a dove in fading Church frescoes, seized upon by unkind popular humour, which is always cruel to divine beings that have had their day.

The Holy Ghost is far less important than that large number of Catholic saints among whom (in contrast to other Catholic ecclesiastical customs) women have equal rights, although only after their death.

The banning of women from active Church service, newly confirmed by Pope Paul VI on 14 September 1972 in true Pauline spirit, invariably sparks off discussion, and yet they seem to steer clear of the core of the matter: The real sin of

77

omission of the Catholic Church is its having damned rather than adopted Eros, the sex god. In cults and mysteries of the old goddesses, he had at least been directed into religious channels where he was able to find his religious outlet. The Church (there was only one at that time) brutally suppressed him, sacrificing hundreds of thousands of 'witches' in the process. Today he is exploding, outside the Church which is powerless to do anything but scold: a belated revenge by Cybele, Ishtar, Atargatis and all the other goddesses. Yet this alone will not cause the death of Christianity. In its present form it will die of itself, of its artificial structure compounded of fact, fiction and the relics of former cults, a structure which is no longer tenable.

In the course of the 'Salzburger Hochschulwochen' (Salzburg University Weeks) of 1972, the well known Catholic dogmatist Professor Josef Finkenzeller of Munich (*cf. Kurier,* Vienna, 8 August 1972) declared that the 'Easter reports' (i.e. the accounts of the resurrection of Jesus) must not be seen as 'history in the sense in which it is known to us'—that is to say, as historical fact—but that they must be understood as *genus litterarium* (belonging to the genre of literature and poetry). With that statement, however, the previous basis of the dogma of redemption is called into question, and all that remains for us is to write an epitaph:

Compared to earlier cults and mythologies Christianity has basically not produced much that is original apart from new names and persons. One celestial 'upper crust' was exchanged for another, while belief in the one God, much-vaunted as progressive vis-à-vis heathendom, can be given only very qualified support. What has remained unconquered is not only Eros, or sexuality, but also the evil in the world. In ancient cults at least an attempt was made to check evil and, through ritual, to get a grip on it, simply by ensuring that the gods appeared in a less moralistic and censorious light.

From the start, Christianity has held itself aloof from this task. It ceded 'this word' to the devil who seemed to be paralysed merely by the resurrection and promise of Christ— at least for the hereafter. But what if this very resurrection is put in doubt? Where then is that which is new, the difference, progress? The era of Christianity is nearing its close. Either it will have to change fundamentally, or gradually vanish, a fate which so far has met all mythologies and religions.

Yet silently in the background, as before, stand the same gods who were once reality and fact. Once again their heritage becomes vacant.

4 The age of miracles

More than just a myth or a religion will die with traditional Christianity. It will represent the end of an era, an age of world history, which from its beginning thousands of years ago has been characterized by the mostly misinterpreted traditions of the cosmic gods, of their sense and essence, their deeds, miracles and implements. An epoch of wrong paths taken, of confused mysticism and superstition which, whatever its form, still obscures our view of the past and the future.

This superstition began at the bottom of the ladder with animals.

A modern Christian will be strangely influenced when he studies old illustrations or sculptures on the pulpits of his churches. For three of the four alleged gospel writers—Mark, Luke and John—are represented as beasts: Mark as a lion, Luke as a bull and John as an eagle. Only Matthew is seen as a man.[1]

Many theologians would be embarrassed if they had to explain this bestialization of men (or humanization of beasts) other than as purely spiritual and symbolical. On no account is it Christian, for a prehistoric stone drawing in Syrian Tel Halaf[2] depicts a hybrid being of eagle, lion and bull, as the prophet Ezekiel saw it later in his visions.

Whenever we may look in the world of the old gods—Egypt, South America, Assur or Babylon—we will see beast-men and men-beasts. There are dog- and jackal-headed gods, gods with the heads of eagles and vultures, lion- and

80

(in India) elephant-shaped gods. The world is a huge zoo, further increased by Christianity: Christ is now serpent, now lion, lamb or eagle,[3] while he later changes into a stork and even into a duck; and in Christian-Ethiopian liturgy his co-regent/mother Mary is worshipped as a holy young heifer.[4]

What lies behind this apparent nonsense which, as was shown in the first chapter by citing the example of the snake, could scarcely be traced back to the idol worship of real animals? For it must be remembered that animals were quite familiar to the people of that period. They were used and eaten exactly as they are today, without consideration for any biological kinship and archetypal components of the soul, which the famous Swiss psychologist C.G. Jung[5] and some of his students and colleagues suspected as the cause of totemism.

The beast of mythology is not the same as that of biological reality. What, then, is it?

We shall attempt to answer this question with the help of the example of the bull, which for millenia has determined and imprinted itself on the cultures of the Mediterranean area.

Pepe Mata was thirty-one and the great hope of Spanish bullfight enthusiasts. They saw him even then as a successor to Dominguin, El Cordobes and others. In August 1971, in the arena of Ciudad Real, he was gored by a bull and died in hospital. Spain mourned Pepe Mata like a folk hero.

Even today, and despite the protests by animal lovers all over the world, the *corrida*, that often lethal combat between man and bull, is an almost sacred affair for a huge number of Spaniards.

The Nobel Prize winner Ernest Hemingway has glorified it in *Death in the Afternoon*, while many scientists have tried to explain the phenomenon with profound psychological theories. In fact, all that is known about bull-fighting is that it goes back to ancient traditions, to Celtic cults and sacrificial rites which in turn can be traced to Crete, where the Minotaur, King Minos' half-man, half-beast creature, lived in the labyrinth until he was killed by Theseus.[6]

However, Egypt and Babylon had the bull-cult too. Attempts have been made to ascribe the veneration of bulls to sexual impulses, but the bull is not as continually ready to copulate as it is generally assumed; any cockerel or rabbit would surpass it in this respect, and yet neither is worshipped as a god because of it.

Why, then, do the Egyptians make such a fuss about their 'Apis'-bull; why do the bull-fights of the Cretans exist; where do the winged bulls of the Babylonians come from? And lastly, why are cattle holy and untouchable in India, while in Spain and South America they are tortured to death in the arena?

At this point, let us fade in a short film, a film from that era when the gods from the Universe had landed on Earth. They come with their arsenal of vehicles and weapons: space gliders, rockets, flying tanks and amphibious tanks which, because of their self-propelled mobility and effect, were regarded as beasts by the natives—dragons, snakes, eagles and winged bulls, depending on their outstanding features. After all, modern war vehicles still bear names like Panther, Tiger, King Tiger, Leopard, etc., while the (peaceful) moon landing-craft of today's astronauts are called Falcon or Spider.

The impression created by such technical marvels on mortals of that time must have been tremendous. Indeed, it was so overwhelming that for thousands of years descriptions of the machines have been handed down with almost eye-witness accuracy. Job of the Old Testament (Job, chapters 40 and 41) reports on the Behemoth and above all the Leviathan as follows:

'His bones *are as* strong pieces of brass[!]; his bones *are* like bars of iron [!]; out of his mouth go burning lamps, *and* sparks of fire leap out. Out of his nostrils goeth smoke, as *out* of a seething pot or caldron . . . a flame goeth out of his mouth. . . .

'The flakes of his flesh are joined together: they are firm in themselves; they cannot be moved. . . .

'He esteemeth iron as straw, *and* brass as rotten wood. The arrow cannot make him flee; slingstones are turned with him into stubble. . . . Sharp stones are under him; he spreadeth sharp pointed things upon the mire. He maketh the deep to boil like a pot of ointment. He maketh a path to shine under him; *one* would think the deep to be *hoary*. . . .'

And the 'God' with whom Job has this dialogue and who makes this pronouncement adds threateningly: 'Shall not *one* be cast down even at the sight of him?'

Later interpreters of the Bible saw in Leviathan a crocodile, a crocodile which makes water boil and 'a path to shine under him'—as if a jet or atomically propelled vehicle had driven over it!

The most frequently used multi-purpose vehicle of the gods seems to have been the 'bull', which was presumably amphibious as well as airworthy, and altogether as versatile as present-day craft. At any rate, the ancient Indian Rig-Veda [7] mentions the 'bulls of magnificent splendour, capable of transformation' (they were obviously beautifully varnished as well); and there is an inscription on the plinth of the statue of Cheruf of the eighteenth Egyptian dynasty [8] which sings of a bull 'that lands safely in its countries when it travels beneath the stars'.

However, there are no bullocks that can be transformed, that shine, fly about the sky and land on the ground!

There is a Hittite legend dating from about the 17th century BC which will finally make the technological nature of these bulls [9] quite clear; in it Asthabi, god of thunder, gives the following orders for the defence against an attack by his Churrithic rival Kumrabi:

'Let the fat be brought, the pure oil. Let the horns of the bull Sherish be anointed with this; let the tail of the bull Tella be covered with gold. Let the mighty rocks be got ready. . .'.

Translated into modern idiom, this is a command for the maintenance personnel to refuel the fighting machines, to oil the protruding barrels of quick-firing weapons (the 'horns') and to activate the bombs (the 'rocks').

The bulls were then ready to take off in the manner of the Egyptian war goddess Sachmet, of whom it is said that her mane(?) smoked, her eyes smouldered with fire, and the desert was clouded with dust when she swished her tail —perhaps the hot exhaust of aero-engines?[10]

Apparently the gods' amphibious flying tanks also contained gas or anaesthetizing weapons, for in the Rig-Veda there is also a report of a 'thousand-horned bull' who came out of the sea, and of whom the anonymous author remarks: 'With the help of this mighty one we send the people to sleep.'

This seems to be the most likely interpretation, particularly when one compares these reports with the considerably more matter-of-fact and sober writings of the Old Testament Jewish prophets who simply call these vehicles 'chariots of the Lord'. An example is the prophet Nahum: 'The chariots [of the Lord] shall rage in the streets, they shall seem like torches, they shall run like the lightnings.' Or the prophet Joel (chapter 2) who says of them that 'they shall walk every one in his path: and *when* they fall upon the sword, they shall not be wounded. They shall run to and fro in the city; they shall run upon the wall, they shall climb up upon the houses. . .'.

According to David in Psalm 68, the god Jehovah disposed of twenty thousand chariots—a Cromwell or Rommel of the past! Here and there the natives of Earth may have attempted to fight the gods' bull-tanks with their primitive weapons; but as a rule they submitted and worshipped them.

This is not as odd as it first appears, for many memorials were erected to the tanks of the victors of 1945; temples were built for the Apis-bulls which were thought to be divine; illustrations from the third millenium BC show one such in the process of destroying the walls of enemy cities.[11]

The cult of the holy bulls which emerged as a result (particularly in the town of Memphis) defies description. During their lifetime the Apis-bulls lived in luxurious apartments in the temple, and the country's most high-born ladies demonstrated their reverence by offering them their bare backs in submission. When finally one of these beasts died of old age, it was embalmed and solemnly buried; in the 13th century BC Rameses II built a special vault which was enlarged by Psammetich I in the 7th century, and ultimately reached a length of 1120 yards.[12,13]

In the same way as the Tibetans would set out to find a new Dalai Lama, the search would begin at once for a worthy successor to the Apis. He had to have certain characteristics: a triangular white mark on the forehead and a crescent-shaped one on the chest or side (Herodotus III:28), or at times the likeness of an eagle on its back. Only then was he considered competent to be a successor.

> Does this not remind us of a modern military parade, with tanks, vehicles and aeroplanes driving and flying past, all bearing similar marks? Displayed on their fronts and flanks will be triangles, squares, stars, rosettes, eagles, etc. Apparently the gods had similar arrangements; military practices seem to be the same throughout the Universe.

For the Egyptian bulls became an unintelligible part of their religion. A bitter farce: tanks became gods, painted emblems turned into sacred marks. The distant 'rattle' of the 'chariot of the Lord' tragically invades our ears. . . .

In India the worship of holy cows reached the height of absurdity, where it has remained to this day. For thousands of years it has been considered the worst of crimes to kill a cow, and to steal one carries the death penalty. The ground on which cows dropped their excreta became holy, and if a man was fortunate enough for a cow to urinate all over him, he too became holy.[14]

The argument that the cult of cows can be traced back to the economic importance of these animals—which in their domestic form were possibly rare to begin with and therefore valuable—can no longer be valid when men are prepared to die of starvation rather than eat them.

Besides, there is a very impressive counter-example recorded by the Greek historian Herodotus: in parts of Egypt it was sometimes the custom to cut off the head of a chosen bull and to fling it onto the nearest dung-heap, accompanied by the most blood-curdling oaths. Thus the bull was not only worshipped as a deity, but also persecuted and hated. This was a fate shared by institutions and symbols of victors and occupying forces at all times, and clearly illustrates that the bull cult was not a procreation or fertility cult, for surely no one would have hated and persecuted any god of that nature.

In this way the phenomenon of those wretched bulls in Spain and South America becomes intelligible. They are first cosseted and fed, and then baited, killed and their dead bodies ignominiously dragged across the sand. These tortured creatures do not know that they die as representatives of and scapegoats for earlier gods. Men no longer know it either; they only sense it and cheer in primitive terror when the god-bull finally goes down and bleeds to death.

The true story of the holy bulls contains a fair amount of the history of man and of religion, and also has a link with the continent of Europe: its name is said to have originated from a Greek maiden who had been deposited on its shores by a bull. It is not surprising that this tale of seduction and abduction has been ascribed to that inveterate Casanova and pursuer of females, Zeus. But what is surprising is that the Olympian king of the gods (usually so dexterous in the use of disguises when bent on yet another seduction) should in this instance turn up disguised as a bull. The shape of a dolphin or a whale would have been more consistent and practical for such a long sea journey as that from Greece to Europe. Yet it was a bull on whose back the maiden Europa travelled to Europe.

The story remains doubtful—unless it conceals something other than one of Zeus's innumerable amorous adventures: possibly something like the distant memory of a planned resettlement of people from the Mediterranean area to the north with the help of amphibious bulls, made of steel, plastic and iron.

There may well have been vehicles capable of such journeys. Homer recounts[15] that the ships of the Phaeacians were made of shining metal, sailing against the wind as swiftly as arrows, and reaching their destination even under cover of night—radar-guided speedboats of antiquity? It is in one of these ships that the Phaeacians are supposed to have taken Odysseus, who had been shipwrecked on their island, back to Ithaca, a journey over hundreds of miles in a single night.

The Nibelung legend also contains reports of such a miraculous ship which glides across the waves without a helmsman and returns the hero Siegfried from Iceland to his home on the Lower Rhine in one day and one night, after his journey to woo Brunhild on behalf of Gunther.[16]

Perhaps the Europeans came to Europe from Atlantis or the Mediterranean in a similar way. If so it would have to have been very early in this history of mankind, approximately at the point when Cro-Magnon Man suddenly appeared in Europe after the end of the last ice age. He already looked something like us, while the indigenous Neanderthal Man was becoming extinct.[17]

It is possible that, hidden in prehistory of this kind, there lies the psychological key to a much later phenomenon: European emigrants setting out for the south and coming to Greece as Dorians and Ionians—returning instinctively, as it were, to their ancient 'home': in the footsteps of the bulls.

History becomes much clearer considered from this aspect. One comes to the disturbing conclusion that all this knowledge must have been lost through the ages.

In the 6th century BC the Greek philosopher Thales of Miletus taught that the stars and the Earth were largely the same in composition. Epicurus declared that there were many inhabited worlds, while Mithrodorus asserted that it was as fatuous to regard the Earth as the sole inhabited world as it was to assume that only one ear of corn would grow in a large cornfield.

Where did this knowledge originate, since there were neither telescopes nor astronomical instruments, and where did it disappear to?

It originated from the knowledge of the gods (generally transmitted only inside secret sects and circles from fear of persecution) *and* from the first beginnings of independent, logical and rational thinking; it has since perished in a flood of stupidity and superstition nurtured by priests and ruling castes, both anxious to retain their dominion.

When the scholar Anaxagoras put forward the thesis in 432 BC that the moon was a fixed heavenly body with

87

mountains, plains and gorges and received its light from the sun, he was accused of heresy and sentenced to death. The sentence was based on a law which had been promulgated by priests shortly before and which rendered all those who did not believe in 'the divine', and who spread new doctrines, liable to prosecution. Anaxagoras saved himself by fleeing the country.[18] His colleague Protagoras, among many others, had expressed doubts about the superhuman divinity of the gods themselves ('. . . and thus I may not know, either that they exist, or that they do not exist') and was banished from Athens, while his writings were publicly burned.[19]

Neither was the Inquisition invented by Christianity.

> *In Greece, then, hundreds of years before the birth of the alleged redeemer of mankind, perhaps mankind's greatest chance was lost—the opportunity of an independent evolution which would be both humanitarian and scientific. The story of this drama has not yet been written.*

After a transitory flickering of a few spiritual sparks, what remains after more than two thousand wasted years is once again no more than superstitious magic, speculation, legend and myth woven round the supposed miracles of the gods.

Did Jesus ever perform miracles? It is hardly likely; at least his miracles were much the same as those performed by other magicians of his time, if one disregards the resurrection and ascension which have been wrongly attributed to him and which are another matter. However, let us discuss the reports in the Bible of miracles which Jesus is said to have performed.

Miracle cures by the laying on of hands and similar practices are nothing new. Aesculapius, Greek god of medicine, had mastered the technique most efficiently— healing people by the use of extended sleep therapy. Slaves who recovered in this way were set free.[20]

Healers and demigods knew how to make the lame walk and the blind see again before and after Jesus. Any Voodoo-magician or medicine-man worthy of the name can do this—at least in the imagination of the people.

The Bible itself shows that Jesus definitely used the methods of medicine in his healing. In John (9:6-7) it is reported that he made a blind man see again by spitting on the ground and treating the eyes with 'the clay', as the Bible has it. The aseptic and healing effect of spittle has been well known for a long time.

Acupuncture, used by the Chinese for more than two thousand years and which at present is being newly discovered in Europe, achieves near-miracles. It is quite certain that Jesus (or rather the authors of his story) would have incorporated this technique too in their miracles tales, had they known it. To this day, practising Christians would have wondered at it still more. . . .

However, the usual healing techniques and tricks were in fact so simple that, according to the Bible, Jesus could soon entrust them to his disciples, whom he sent out in pairs to recruit new supporters and to perform miracles. They were 'commanded that they should take nothing for *their* journey'—a remarkable allusion—'no money in their purse', and not 'two coats', but a staff (Mark 6:8-9). One may recollect that metal (money, buttons etc.) may be either a hindrance or a danger under certain circumstances when using magical effects; but above all it reminds us of the magic wand. Its function was no longer understood by the gospel writers; this is illustrated in Matthew (10:10) where the disciples are told that they must have 'nor yet staves': obscure matters were rendered in obscure language. On the other hand, Christ's instructions that his recruiting team were not to linger in any town where they were not welcome ('shake off the dust under your feet') are rather worldly-modern and not at all lovingly-gracious. They were told to travel on—'time is money'—and console themselves with the thought that 'It shall be more tolerable for Sodom and Gomorrha in the day of judgment, than for that city.' But Sodom and Gomorrha had *already* fared badly.

Now, the twelve (in Luke they are seventy) recruiters for salvation set out, casting out 'many devils', and 'anointed with oil[!] many that were sick' (Mark 6:13). Which brings

89

us back to the universal miracle healing oil of the gods!

The magic becomes more interesting and different when Jesus is 'transfigured' before the disciples Peter, James and John, and apparently even conjures up the dead, as in Mark 9:2-9. In this report it says that Jesus had taken the three 'into a high mountain', where his 'raiment became shining, exceeding white as snow; so as no fuller on earth can white them. . .'.

Whereupon Elias and Moses appeared and 'were talking with Jesus'.

The three disciples were 'sore afraid', above all when 'there was a cloud that overshadowed them' and also when that well known voice from 'out of the cloud' announced: 'This is my beloved Son: hear him.'

Here the Oriental-Christian story-tellers have mixed up a large number of uncomprehended 'magical' matters:

> *The becoming 'exceeding white as snow' corresponds to the external optical effect of a divine transformation. Quetzalcoatl, Sido and other gods became white and shining during this process.*
>
> *The appearance of phantoms which the disciples take for Moses and Elias corresponds to reproductions and duplications during bodily transformation of an intense physical nature; some idea of this process will be conveyed by the analogy of the double image on the screen of a badly-adjusted television set.*
>
> *The 'cloud' has been a well known part of divine manifestation ever since Moses: it is the smoke from the vehicles of the gods, and the voice comes through a loudspeaker.*

Jesus probably did not have the least connection with all these manifestations: he never climbed up any sacred mountain where phenomena of that nature may have been visible to the eyes of 'mortals' thousands of years ago.

It was the unknown authors of the Gospel of St Mark who gathered all this, lumping it together until it was so unintelligible that they were themselves seized with horror (because they understood nothing of it); in consequence, after the event they made Jesus say (Mark 9:9) that 'they should tell no man what things they had seen, till the Son of man were risen from the dead.'

Did Jesus really conjure up the spirits of Moses and Elias? Hardly—neither could he have done so, since Elias as well as Moses are similarly only names for persons who probably never lived (and even if they did live, it was in quite a different manner).[21]

Much more tangible and realistic in comparison is the story of the raising of Lazarus, which is described in detail in the Gospel of St John (11:1-44).

Lazarus was the brother of Mary, one of the women following Jesus (not to be confused with the mother of Jesus). Lazarus had died and had already been lying in his grave for four days—'Lord, by this time he stinketh', remarked his relative, Martha—before Jesus could at last be persuaded to go there. The dead man was buried in a cave (as was Jesus, too, at a later date), 'and a stone lay upon it'. Jesus ordered the stone to be removed, and called Lazarus by his name; and he came forth, 'bound hand and foot with grave-clothes', like an Egyptian mummy. Strangely enough we are not told what happened to the reanimated Lazarus; it merely says Jesus had ordered: 'Loose him and let him go.'

Two explanations are feasible: either Jesus was operating some sort of magic, some mass hypnotism, like an Indian fakir with his rope-trick; or (and this seems more likely) the gospel writer took over the whole story from the mythology of earlier gods' resurrections. This mythology contains all the essential features which we see again later during the alleged resurrection of Jesus himself: the grave, the special wrapping of the corpse, the stone in front of the grave (the door of the transformation autoclave), and the call, the acoustic activation of the transformation machinery. The strict adherence to the three- to four-day period is typical almost to the point of constituting circumstancial evidence.

Jesus knows that Lazarus is dead (John 11:14), but he takes his time—indeed, the relatives are convinced that by this time the corpse would be likely to stink. He must adhere to that period, for it corresponds to the instructions issued by the gods for the process of transformation, the point being that it takes that long for a person about to be transformed to be ready, or 'well done'.

It is clear, too, that the Lazarus resurrection story also is not a historic event, but a borrowing from the gods by the writer of the Gospel of St John.

The other evangelists did likewise. They obtained whatever they could from the great magical box of the gods and heaped it all on Jesus, and in this they were not one bit more unscrupulous than the sensational reporters of today.

Weather-making and dominion over wind, rain and sea, as mentioned in Matthew (8:26)—Jesus 'rebukes' the wind and the sea, 'and there was a great calm'—are ancient skills wielded by the gods. It was known to Frau Hulda in Germany (the 'Frau Holle' of Grimms' fairy-tale fame) as well as to the Toltec weather-god Tlaloc and to the god Si of the Peruvian Simu tribe. [22] Of course, the historic Jesus never rebuked or commanded storms or weather, just as the biblical Moses never parted the Red Sea with a magic wand. These are merely memories of similar practices of the gods, practices which today we begin to imitate on a modest scale by using aeroplanes to 'milk' clouds with the help of dry ice and silver iodide crystals, or by clearing fog from runways with radio-beam devices.

Jesus walks 'on the sea' (to mention yet another of the alleged miracles), and in so doing manages to join his disciples who had preceded him in a boat (Matt. 14:25-6). In the same way Hermes, the Greek messenger of the gods, walked or flew over land and sea on 'winged shoes'. [23] It is interesting that it was on winged shoes, and not with wings on his back— could this have been a flying craft of a kind unknown to us? Or perhaps it is a memory of the fact that the gods (as Homer hinted when he called them 'light-footed' and thought one could easily recognize them by the movement of their legs and feet) [24] that these gods possibly came from planets with *different gravity conditions*. They may have been able to go about literally in leaps and bounds, sometimes even over water, just like today's astronauts on the moon.

A copy of a rock drawing of the Iranian god Ahura Mazda on the rock of Behistan in Persia. The drawing illustrates who this god is: not a winged being, but a man in the process of entering or leaving a flying machine. His wings, unlike those in bowdlerized and distorted depictions of Christian angels, do not sprout from his shoulders – they are not part of his body. Equally clearly visible are what may well be landing skids or landing wheels, as well as in his left hand a steering wheel, since we cannot assume that Ahura Mazda has temporarily removed his 'halo'!

Temple entrance at Abu Simnel in Egypt. Here, as with temple and gate structures in Central and South America, the same features are displayed: the side and upper parts are massive; the gates and doors, however, are very small and narrow. Why did the architects of those days build such narrow openings when doubtless they had the skill to do otherwise?

Transformers at a modern high-tension plant. At the top of the next page is a depiction of a 'moon column' from the Near East. The similarity is startling. Could it be that these and other sacred pillars were nothing less than later imitations of energy installations?

What are we to think of columns which taper from top to bottom, like those at the palace of Knossus on Crete?

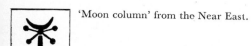

'Moon column' from the Near East.

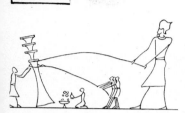

In the Egypt of the 18th dynasty (16th to 14th centuries BC) the so-called DED pillar was considered sacred. It was both a character and a protective symbol, the 'spine of Osiris'. This is still a mystery. Many scholars have taken it to be a defoliated tree, but this is not very likely. In our picture (*left*) a DED pillar is being erected, apparently by a god (or pharaoh) with the help of human workers. Was the DED pillar a technical implement?

'And when he thus had spoken, he cried with a loud voice, Lazarus, come forth. And he that was dead came forth, bound hand and foot with grave clothes: and his face was bound about with a napkin.' (John 11: 43–4.) There are many reports of magicians and miracle-workers of that period raising people from the dead: it is an echo of the 'resurrection in the flesh' which the gods were capable of performing long ago.

In temple buildings there are one or more chambers (*cellae*) surrounded by pillars. They form the nave (*naos*), and in front of this is the *pronaos*. Where do these nautical terms come from? Temples were not ships, nor were they in any way copies of ships. It seems more likely that there was some connection with the sky-travellers, or astro-'nauts'; they went into the 'naos' in order to travel to the stars, while their technicians manipulated their instruments in the 'opistodomos', the control chamber. Today it is taken as a matter of course that in the old days temples were erected to the gods – but nobody has asked why.

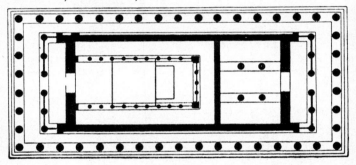

Ground-plan of the cathedral at Mayence. Its characteristics are similarly pillars, main room, altar area and sacristy (instrument and control room).

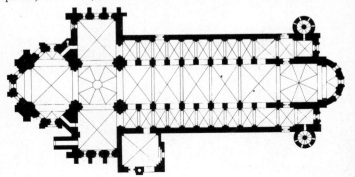

Illustrations of shod feet scratched into rocks at Simrisham in Sweden have baffled investigators to this day.

At Cholula in Mexico in the autumn of 1519, Spaniards under the command of Hernando Cortez burned local leaders at the stake. (From Las Casas, 'True Report of the Spaniards', 1613.)

A Cretan priestess. The snakes in her hands are symbols of transformation
and ascension. Later the snake is also found in Christian symbolism: Mary,
Queen of Heaven, crushes its head.

From the tombs of the Kings of Ur: the alleged hero Gilgamesh holding two bulls in his arms, both of which stare as stupidly as he does. The bulls' human faces are a clear indication of the confusion caused by giving animal names to certain vehicles and flying craft of the gods with their human occupants.

J. F. Blumrich, a leading scientist at NASA, has declared Ezekiel's chariot of God to be the reactor-driven landing-craft of an extra-terrestrial spaceship.

A papyrus illustration of the ancient Egyptian goddess Nut. Her star-studded body symbolically encompasses the vault of the heavens and the world.

The interesting point is this: In the drawing there are nine illustrations of the Key of the Nile – two of them hanging from the hands of the figure sitting in the centre. The Key of the Nile was the emblem of life, the representation of a 'sacred implement' which must have been of the most tremendous significance and is represented today in bishops' croziers. Was it a weapon or an all-purpose laser-beam emitter?

It was probably both, for otherwise it would never have been emphasized to such a degree, and what is more, in connection with the stars, the sky, and the gods.

Two 'rods of Hermes' from Greece. The stylized serpents are a symbol of resurrection (i.e. of a changing of skin) or, more probably, depictions of energy conductors. The wings indicate the divine provenance of the rods.

The coat of arms of the Swiss canton of Basle and (identical in every detail) of Sweden. It represents a stylized crozier which has here been deliberately laid on its side. Thus its true function is clearly a device, a weapon. On the left is the grip (butt-end); in front of that are the trigger rings (or energy, or cooling, rings) and the stylized 'explosion'.

Questions like these ought not be dismissed as speculation or ancient superstition. The Greeks (or at least their scholars and philosophers) were much less superstitious than many are today. Plato (427-347 BC), in his work concerning the State,[25] says of the gods: 'They behave like magicians, but in reality they are quite natural.'

Plato, of course, did not know the former cosmic gods in person; at the most he knew distant descendants of theirs. But from information he had gathered in Egypt he knew considerably more about them than we do today; certainly he knew more than any chaplain or parson, who has only the vaguest idea about such things and about physics, and who is expected to report on the alleged miraculous deeds of a man who lived and died nineteen hundred years ago. Moreover, how is it possible for a clergyman, who has been reared and educated in the conviction that the Bible is the only true annunciation and revelation of God, to judge objectively that very Bible and its contents?

He cannot do it. In a still worse way, though, are those believers who must swallow as Holy Writ a confused hotch-potch of facts, misunderstandings and inventions which editors, thirty, fifty or two hundred years after the alleged events, had mixed together. What is essentially tragi-comic in this context is that the real gods of the Universe probably never thought in terms of performing miracles nor of having a miraculous effect on others. So it was not their fault if the Earth dwellers looked upon the clothing and equipment of the extra-terrestrial visitors (especially their helmets, masks, breathing apparatus, antennae, etc.) as animal forms, and drew them as such—after all, they had no other means of comparison.

An example serves to show how this may have come about. An unknown Chinaman—not from prehistoric times but in AD 1839—has drawn an English sailor as he saw him: a smoke-belching monster with the head of a bird and claws for hands and feet. Perhaps it was fear and xenophobia that guided his pencil, and there is no reason why this should not have also frequently happened long ago.

The same may be applied to relatively simple technical

implements used by the temporary divine occupation force and which were regarded as magic charms.

How many drivers are there who have not the faintest idea of how their car works, and who would not be in the least surprised if under the bonnet, instead of four or six cylinders, there were four or six dwarfs looking after the propulsion? What's the difference?!

It might have been a matter of course for the gods to use wireless and loudspeaker installations for the announcements of their orders and commands, especially since they were few in number and unable to be everywhere at the same time. These would certainly have been constructed like ours, although they may have looked different. Perhaps, though, they did not look that much different: we need only glance at any sports stadium or hall where mass meetings are held to see steel pillars topped by loudspeakers announcing competition results. If we then make our way to the ancient Egyptian department of the technological museum of the gods and view exhibits five, six or seven thousand years old, we see the famous 'talking pillars' of the god Thot (who later became Hermes *trismegistos*, the 'thrice-great'. Through these he gave advice and pronounced wise sayings to the people, just as today Chairman Mao pronounces his Thoughts.[26] That is why he was called 'Thot of the pillar'.

These particular pillars, or loudspeaker supports, must not be confused with the columns and supporting pillars in temples, which were imitations of high-tension poles and insulators.

Speaking pillars were usually made of iron, such as the two which stood in the courtyard of the temple built by Solomon in Jerusalem (Josephus Flavius, VIII, 3-4). They had a kind of 'head' and were surrounded by a 'trellis-work of brazen palm trees'—probably the symbolized cables of the loudspeakers.

There were 'iron trees which revealed all the mysteries' on various sacred peaks of the Himalayas and in Himalayan caves.[27] Similarly, the sacred Irminsul of the ancient Germans, which was destroyed in the 8th century AD, [28] might have originated from the radio-loudspeaker installa-

94

tions of the gods; as might the well known statue of the Slavic god Swantewit on the Isle of Rügen, which the Danish king Waldemar had overturned and which boasted four 'heads' (=copies of loudspeakers): according to reports by the historian 'Saxo grammaticus', it was partly made from 'precious metals', and transmitted forecasts about the forthcoming harvest and similar matters.[29]

It is characteristic of the essentially technical method of transmitting divine orders and commands to the people—whether they were made from pillars, robots, or loudspeaker-carrying vehicles and aeroplanes—that, as Moses and the prophets repeatedly reported, the 'voice of the Lord' was often terribly loud, like 'the voice of the trumpet' (Exod. 19:16). We might say that the loudspeakers were not properly adjusted. Now Daniel was addressed by an angel—not, though, from a pillar, but from out of a robot ('his body also was like the beryl . . . his arms and his feet like in colour to polished brass. . . ' (Dan. 10:9)). Daniel immediately faints as a result of the noise: 'Yet heard I the voice of his words: and when I heard the voice of his words, then was I in a deep sleep on my face, and my face toward the ground.' (Dan. 10:9) Apparently the sound waves were so strong that the poor fellow felt that 'my comeliness was turned in me into corruption, and I retained no strength.' (Dan. 10:8) His companions at this interview had crept away just in time.

It is hard to describe the effect of supersonic apparatus more clearly. However, it will at best have been 'inner voices' that the numerous Christian 'pillarites' heard who later took to squatting on the remains of ancient pillars, only to go to ruin through a completely misunderstood recollection of the speaking pillars: for the pillars on which they squatted definitely never spoke a word. Finally, a very last mythical relic of the speaking pillars and heads can be found in enigmatic reports of the Christian Order of the Temple, whose knights were said to have possessed a head of brass, the 'Baphomet', which spoke and prophesied. On this account, and also because their views and teachings often clashed with those of the Mother Church, they were prohibited by Pope Clement V in 1312 and their order dissolved.

It is impossible to say whether the Templars did in fact have what might have been a 'people's radio receiver' belonging to the gods, one that had survived for thousands of years; but even if they did have one in the shape of the Baphomet, it would have been absolutely worthless, since in those days no god was any longer alive and transmitting.

This applies too to the time of Moses, and yet he agitated against the iron speaking pillars of his tribal god Jehovah's predecessors and competitors: 'Ye shall destroy their altars, and break down their images [=pillars]' (Deut. 7:5), never suspecting that imitations of such pillars would later stand in the sanctuary of the Hebrews. This is understandable if one considers that the Jews were dragging around a similar miracle-working device—the legendary Ark of the Covenant which was supposedly used by Moses to communicate with his chief.

A great deal has been written and conjectured about this box which was approximately 5 feet long and 2½ feet wide and high. Moses and his assistants fashioned it out of 'shittim wood' and gold, following the do-it-yourself instructions given by Jehovah. This box, with its complicated rings, staves and borders, probably represents an electrical installation, as is apparent from the equally precise operating instructions and the numerous warnings about 'unauthorized trespassers'. In the Old Testament an accident is graphically described (2 Sam. 6:6-7): While it was being transported on a cart, the Ark threatened to slip to the ground because the oxen shook it; a man called Uzzah took hold of it to steady it, or rather he tried to, for at the same moment he fell down dead: an early victim of electric shock. Anything else about the Ark is likely to be either recklessly exaggerated or simply adopted from earlier reports about *genuine* technical devices used by the gods. Both the Ark of the Covenant (in its function as magical box) and the holy pillars which existed at that time (13th and 12th centuries BC) were at best amateurish copies, toys which more or less simulated their models but were unable to replace them.

For the 'children', the people of that era, this might have

been quite sufficient. It certainly was for the priests: with the help of occasional *coups de théâtre*, such as the lightning effects of the Ark, they kept their flock at heel and themselves in full enjoyment of power, a power which had been usurped by their presumptuous succession of the gods—by using 'miracles'.

> *There is need of serious discussion as to whether belief in miracles does in fact represent a human need, as is so often asserted, or whether it has not rather been thrust upon the people.*
> *Miracles are nothing but uncomprehended reality.*

If the gods were to visit Earth today with all their vehicles, devices and technical arsenal, we might admire and acknowledge them politely, but we would quite definitely not regard them as miraculous and magical. Indeed, we are no longer even disturbed by such manifestations of the other world as clairvoyance or ghosts, because we have come to recognize them as higher-dimensional psi energies, which we are beginning to manipulate.

We no longer wonder at anything, and in this respect we have come to be like the gods.

And that is the ultimate reason why all forms of belief, and all religions which are based on miracles, are doomed to die: they are mummies which may possibly remain effective for a time, but which are basically already museum-pieces.

In the gods' museum of technological history there are a number of exhibits similar to the Ark of the Covenant or the loudspeaker pillars which long ago were considered holy and miraculous. In part they are represented today in symbolic form, as in the curved pastoral staff—the crozier—of bishops and popes. It is an emblem which has nothing in common with the simple crook used by humble shepherds, but very much with the 'miracle rods' of prehistoric times, used by the gods and conferred by them on their vassals and favourites as 'lend-lease' weapons.

One such is the Egyptian Key of the Nile, depicted in innumerable illustrations. Another is the rod of Thyrsos that

97

belonged to Hermes, with the help of which the most amazing miracles could be performed. This was an object 3 to 4 yards long. 'Serpents' (presumably cables) were coiled round it, and a special feature was a red ring.[30]

This portentous ring can be found in illustrations dating from the third millenium BC.[31] Was it a release ring, a trigger? It would seem quite feasible when one learns that the Greek god Hermes received such a device from his divine brother Apollo. With it he was able to 'close the eyes of the mortals' (for 'close' read 'anaesthetize') (Homer: *Iliad*, 343) The Egyptian-Greek god Dionysus also owned such a magic rod. He 'paralysed' the giant Eurytus with it, and men stood in great dread of it. It is said to have been made of a metal which shone like gold.[32]

Moses performed many miracles with a staff of the gods. He made water flow out of a rock and divided the Red Sea for the Israelites fleeing from Egypt ('But lift thou up thy *rod* and stretch out thine hand over the sea, and divide it. . . .' (Exod: 14:16) And the sea supposedly divided, just as, according to an Indian legend, the mountains of the Kashmir Valley divided when the hero Cashyab set about them with a magical golden (!) sword.[33]

Today, when scientists are at work on the construction of portable laser weapons, none of this seems miraculous any longer: at most it is a dire portent of the future.

In mythology, magic and miracle-rods undergo many transformations. They become the stick of Hades, god of the Underworld, and the magic cudgel of Heracles (Pindar: *Olympic Odes*, 9). The Roman magician-priests, the Augurs, used them for their mumbo-jumbo.[34] Bishops, emperors and marshals still hold them in their hands in stylized form. But so powerful, so deeply programmed in the minds of men are that dread of and reverence for this healing or destroying implement, that over the centuries they have willingly submitted to the bearers of these emblems of power. Last but not least, a degenerate form of magic rod is the broomstick on which witches rode to their assemblies.

Similarly the magician's 'magic wand', that most important of requisites in any child's cheap box of tricks, is hardly 'an elongated finger', as sophisticated psychologists have attempted to interpret it. It is simply a primitive form of a technical device which in the era of the gods was very real and very effective.

If these deductions appear fantastic (they are in fact quite the opposite), consider where the rings on the bishops' croziers came from (incidentally, in the coat of arms of the Swiss canton of Basle they are particularly prominent). They are beneath the upper curved part, what was presumably the original butt or grip of the implement. They seem to be quite useless, a mere ornament. . . .

But might they not be a remnant of those red rings, the release rings on the rods and weapons of the gods, which were so frequently mentioned many thousand years earlier? That, at any rate, would be a logical explanation.

There is one positively classic exhibit in our miraculous museum of the gods. For once, it is a peaceful and harmless object: the ladder, or rope-ladder.

In the imagination of Jews and Christians alike it became a holy-mystical 'ladder of heaven' thanks to the biblical Jacob, who recounted his dream of a ladder: 'The top of it reached to heaven: and behold the angels of God ascending and descending on it.' (Gen. 28:12)

There are plenty of people flying through the sky today—airplane pilots and passengers, for instance, or astronauts moving about in space outside their spaceships. Long before Jacob it would seem to have been very similar; according to pyramid texts from the 3rd century BC,[35] the dead Egyptians climbed up to heaven on *rope-ladders*. The matter could be said to be established as fact in an oracular text found in the temple of Heracles at Eritrea[36,37] commanding women to plait their hair into ropes and ladders, for then a boat of the gods would follow them—meaning that this might be a way of coming into contact with one.

There are many legends all over the world about gods who came to Earth down ropes and ladders—Quat, the Melanesian bringer of culture,[38] for instance. It is often reported that the gods brought people threatened by floods or fire to safety

99

with the aid of ropes and 'baskets' which were lowered by 'spiders'; such a traditional tale existed, for example, among the North American Yana Indians.[39]

Obviously neither the Yana legend-teller nor a certain Herr Müller (when he was writing his doctoral thesis in 1930) were in a position to visualize what we can today:

> One need only look at a helicopter or one of the astronauts' landing craft to realize immediately what might have been meant by the 'spiders' of the gods; and anybody who has seen the recovery of moon explorers from the Pacific on television will know what the threads and baskets of spiders were all about.

Now we begin to understand why, even long after the gods had left, the Indians on the plateau of Nazca in Peru made gigantic scratch drawings on the ground, depicting spiders, birds and similar animals. These were their symbols and concepts of the gods' vehicles, and the purpose of the drawings was apparently to signal to them: 'Here is a place for you to touch down, return to us!' Jacob's Ladder, then, was an ordinary ladder made of light alloy or rope, while the 'Lord' who could be seen standing high up in the clouds was probably the commander of the flying vehicle to which it belonged.

It would be hardly possible to investigate in detail the legacy of the gods. It can be found everywhere and at all times, occasionally in a ridiculously obvious form. For example, there is the story told by the ancient Germans of how Siegfried, returning from Iceland and arriving at one of his castles in the land of the Nibelungs, tried to get in. The castle was guarded by a giant, apparently a robot. Siegfried knocked at the gate, but presumably he used an incorrect code, for the giant failed to identify his master and attacked him. It took Siegfried a great deal of effort to switch him off, or 'vanquish' him. Of course, one asks why a guard who had been left behind should not have recognized his master; the answer is because he was not a living man, but a machine, capable of reacting only to certain impulses.

In the same legend Siegfried, in order to overcome the athletic Brunhild on behalf of Gunther, his liege lord, takes a ring from her after a bout of nocturnal free-style wrestling. (Brunhild is now so weak that she must surrender even to flyweight Gunther.) This was one of those magic rings mentioned in so many legends and technically similar to the magic girdle of the dwarf king Laurin—it gave him super-human strength, until Theoderic the Great saw through his trick and defeated him.[40]

The 'magic hood' plays an important role in these fights. It made the wearer invisible, which is something which gives headaches to modern technological engineers, even though invisibility through diverting light by means of magnetic fields is theoretically possible. Apparently the 'dwarfs', predecessors of the gods on Earth, knew the trick, for all magic hoods mentioned in legends were created by them.

There now remains the dragon, strange beast of fable and fairy tale. That Nordic superman Siegfried had an epic fight with one. According to one of the many versions of the legend, the monster looked something like this:

'It was pitch-black with blue wings. Ponderous in flight, it vigorously curled its long tail'—in the manner of the Loch Ness Monster, perhaps.

'From its nostrils flashed blue flames which would kill the hero's dogs, and from its inside there could be seen a fiery glow.'[41]

The dwarf accompanying Siegfried took to his heels with the help of his magic hood as soon as he saw the dragon, while his master had great trouble in defeating the monster.

In the end it was consumed by its own heat. This dragon must have been some sort of jet helicopter which Siegfried 'shot' with his miraculous sword (= ray gun?), and which subsequently exploded and crashed in flames.

There is little likelihood of anything like a saurian or crocodile ever having existed capable of emitting blue flames or 'consuming itself in its own heat' at the moment of death.

Most of the dragons of myth and legend were not living animals, nor did they represent some metaphorical backward glance at prehistoric saurians (for they had quite different qualities). Rather they were machines—flying appliances and vehicles of the gods, just like the legendary bull. This explains why the dwarfs, normally a malicious breed, actually helped human beings in their struggle against these objects. They hated the gods who had arrived after them, for they had been turned into ridiculous dwarfs only by the propagandist distortion of those same later immigrants from space; they had been forced to retreat as underground fighters to their final bases beneath the surface of the earth—to the caves of the Rosengarten in the southern Tyrol, for instance.

Seen from this angle the fairy tales of history turn into one huge, homogeneous drama, to a very normal and human tragedy. The holy dragon-slayer George, for example, is now no longer a pious legend but a figure from an ancient battle report.

The above-mentioned magic rings and girdles were no more than mini control gear for energy instruments, similar to those used by moon explorers and for the purpose of steering one-man torpedo planes. Fundamentally the technique is always the same and must remain so, whether on Earth or on other planets.

If that seems exaggerated, then consider this:

> *How could people ever have thought of any ring, girdle or bracelet giving special powers and abilities to the wearer unless they had, at some stage, seen and experienced this? How, in any case, did they come to wear such objects at all?*

Any explanation favouring the imitation and further development of examples and behaviour patterns in animals is open to doubt. It might possibly explain the fact that savages daub themselves with paint or enhance and adorn their genitals— but not the use of jewellery.

There *are* animals which use tools—some woodpeckers hold thorns in their beaks with which to poke about in the bark of trees, impaling worms and maggots on them, while anthropoid apes can join bamboo rods together and use them as tools or weapons. But there is not a single known animal

102

which wears artificial 'jewellery'.

> *Necklaces, bracelets on wrists and ankles, girdles and finger-rings are not natural phenomena. They were neither taken over by animals in their evolutionary process, nor were they invented by men merely for fun. In accordance with their form and meaning, they are a copy of certain components of the garments or implements used by the gods.*

In that context, neck-rings would correspond to the bulge of the fastening on space helmets, bracelets on wrists and ankles to the cuffs on flying suits, ear-rings would symbolize head-phones, and girdles and finger-rings, as explained above, switch gear, watches, etc.

The original significance of the ring, for example, can scarcely be supposed to have been based on its imaginary *material value*, but on its *function* as a switching (and hence magic) device; to make it work it always had to be twisted first.[42] The ring, 'sanctified' through its divine origins, was thus a symbol of power. The rings of popes and bishops are still reverently kissed today. Eminent personalities are distinguished by gifts of rings of honour. The ring has retained its magic, even though knowledge of its meaning has long been forgotten.

Similarly gold, whose value for practical applications is no greater than any other material, nonetheless played a part in the domination of thought and action, economy and politics, for thousands of years. It still does so, in spite of Lenin's assertion that, at best, it would be used to line urinals in the society of the future.

Lenin was not the first to despise gold. The Incas viewed it with contempt, although (or because) they possessed large quantities of it. When their King Atahualpa saw how his Spanish visitors eagerly grabbed all the gold they could lay their hands on, he ordered them to be given 5000 tons of it, probably in the hope that it would make them go away. The Spaniards did not go away, however, but wanted still more, so the Inca people had to die for the gold which, although

103

they did use it themselves, they called contemptuously 'excrement of the Gods'.[43]

Why was it that, for these and other ancient American peoples, gold was on the one hand 'sacred', and on the other hand 'excrement'?

The answer provides the key to the understanding of the disastrous magic of gold: We learn from a number of traditions[44],[45] that the cosmic gods had used a material which very much resembled, but was not in fact, gold for their vehicles, tools and buildings. The Greeks and other ancient peoples still realized there was a difference: they called the 'gold of the gods' *oreichalkos* (literally 'mountain ore') in contrast to earthly metals (*chalkos*). It was the 'red gold', often mentioned by Homer, allegedly lighter than the earthly metal and possessing other qualities. To the gods it was as commonplace as steel or plastic are to us, whereas to mortals it was something special, and since they had none of it, they put their own earthly gold in its place. Yet it is not to the latter, but to the multi-purpose metal of the gods, that all the legends of miraculous golden swords and daggers and so on refer; and had they in fact been made of real gold, they would have been of no practical use at all.

The last traces of this gold-like divine material seem to have been preserved for a surprisingly long time. The Greek historian Plutarch (AD 64—125) reports in *De Iside et Osiride* that, a few decades prior to his visit to Egypt, remains of reddish-gold material were to be found on one of the islands of the Nile; it had come from that 'ship of Osiris' in which the god had travelled to Earth from heaven, the 'sea of the night'. At this time, he remarked, it was worth more than gold.

Plato, Plutarch's fellow-countryman and predecessor, was able to narrate that the roofs in the capital of the mysterious island kingdom of Atlantis had been covered with this same *oreichalkos*, the gold of the gods.

It was man's mania for imitation which later led him to cover the roofs and turrets of temples, palaces and mosques with 'gold'. The world-famous Goldenes Dachl (Golden Roof) at Innsbruck, for example, is in this context a pale reflection of far-distant divine splendour.

Gold, like most things that originated from the gods, is an error, a misunderstanding. Perhaps somewhere in the next world, Atahualpa and Lenin are having a good laugh. . . .

For there is no apparent reason why gold and gold alone, and not some other material, has become the measure of all things—other than through imagination and the wrongly understood imitation of the gods.

Even today the strength and vigorousness of the impulses and programmings of that age of miracles and magic can be seen by any open-minded person who visits a Catholic church. Here (and to some extent in a Protestant church) there is a large selection of things representing the gods' technical achievements:

The classic church building, from Cologne Cathedral to the simple village church, corresponds in design to a temple with its holy gate (after passing it one removes one's hat), pillars, nave, altar area and sacristy. Here we have the modified energy-transformation gate; the traditional high-tension and transformer pillars; the sepulchre (or furnace) of the gods (represented by the altar) and the appropriate pieces of machinery (the high altar) and the control room behind it. Steps and protective grilles separate believers from the 'holy' (dangerous) area. The message, or 'word', is proclaimed from the pulpit, which is often adorned with the animal emblems of the spacemen-gods. It is reached by a 'Jacob's Ladder'. For it was from above, whether from mountains or from flying vehicles, that the gods used to speak to the people.

In the spires which reach to the sky in an attempt to copy the gods' rockets, the brazen bells are ringing, and have been doing so since prehistory (e.g. in China).[56] They summon the believers to prayer and chase away evil spirits, just as Heracles did when he chased away and

105

destroyed the Stymphalids (hostile gods' flying machines) with 'brazen clappers' [47] *—reminders of the ultrasonic weapons being reinvented today.*

As the service begins, sacristans (assistants) appear in white assistants' smocks. (It would seem that these garments have never undergone any changes at all.) They accompany the priest, or chief technician of the imminent transformation ceremony, to the gods' furnace-sepulchre-table, the altar, and produce the smoke that clouded around both the Tabernacle of Moses and the energy-transfer devices of the gods. At regular intervals they ring small bells (similar signal bells may have rung when a god was about to transform himself). The priest himself wears specially-designed robes (protective garments) to guard against possible radiation, and when he lifts his hands (in warning), or shows the congregation the magically-transformed body of God, the believers hide their faces in their hands. (This is the recommended procedure during outbreaks of atomic radiation. That this is a definite protective gesture may be confirmed in Exodus (33:20) where the God Jehovah of Moses warns : '. . .for there shall no man see me, and live.')

When the symbolic act of sacrifice has been successfully completed, the sacrificed god is eaten (and possibly also drunk) by the believers. Then the priests and assistants stow away the transformation devices again (in accordance with the safety regulations of the holy books) and change their garments. If a bishop is present, he of course carries his (miraculous) crozier and (miraculous) ring, and on his head wears the mitre (barely recognizable as a helmet, reminding us of the bull-head ornaments of Egyptian deities).

There is not one single detail in this religious rite which cannot be attributed in one way or another to the imitation of the behaviour and techniques of the gods.

This tradition begins with the christening with water—i.e.

with the immersion and re-emergence of the person to be baptized. Jehova's Witnesses still carry it out in its original form today; the astronauts do too, indirectly, each time they splash down in the Pacific.

At the time of Jesus of Nazareth, John the Baptist supposedly lived on the banks of the Jordan, baptizing people by immersing them in the river and quoting the words of the prophet Isaiah: 'Prepare ye the way of the Lord, make his paths straight.' (Matt. 3:3)

Why should people immerse themselves in water, and whose 'paths' are they helping to prepare?

The answer to this, and the explanation for an otherwise unintelligible action, lies, literally, with the gods. When they first arrived on Earth they immersed themselves in the water in their spaceships as a precaution and then came to the surface. The god of the Peruvians, Kon Isla Tc'hsi Huira-cocha, landed in Lake Titicaca;[48] the Sun God landed near the Pacific Caroline Islands;[49] near Tahiti, a 'giant bird' laid a 'metal egg' in the sea;[50] the 'egg of Helena' came down on the Euphrates;[51] and the lovely Aphrodite herself came out of the sea, which is why she was called *anadyomène* ('she who emerges from the water').

As they came down from heaven, gods plunged into the water and emerged again: man is merely emulating them.

Whether the idea of a symbolic cleansing with water has also played a role in baptism is a moot question. It was probably attributed to it later on, when no other explanation could be found.

Baptism is the first of the Christian sacraments (literal translation: sanctities, oaths). The Catholics possess seven sacraments and the Protestants two. Not one of them appears to have originated from the historic Jesus; this claim was 'decided upon' as dogma only about four hundred years ago at the Council of Trent (1545-63). All so-called sacraments are imitations of 'divine' models, including the last one that a practising Catholic receives: Extreme Unction. Despite zealous revisions by many authors, no mention is made of this in the entire New Testament. Where, then, does it come from?

Well, even in ancient Egypt the god Osiris was oiled and anointed before his death;[52] and statues of the Greek god Hermes and other deities were 'anointed with shining oil'—not only in the West, but also in Asia, Africa and India.

But what has oil, or for that matter grease of any sort, to do with a man's 'last journey'? Why were the images of the gods oiled and anointed? Why the significance of oil in a machineless era? Or could it be that there were machines, after all?

We shall have to go back a long time, five or six thousand years, to the time when the Sumerian epic of Gilgamesh was first recorded in writing. There are several versions of this oldest of epic stories, just as there are of the Siegfried and Christ legends.[53,54,55]

They all contain the previously-mentioned fight with the celestial beast which is defeated by the hero Gilgamesh and his companion Enkidu. The story continues: After the fight, Gilgamesh hands the 'horns' of the monster, which had been sent into action against him by the goddess Ishtar, to the armourers of Uruk (Gilgamesh Epic, tablet VI, 172-3). The horns are described in detail. They were made of lapis lazuli (glass fibre), 2 inches thick and together contained 6 kor of oil. (According to A. Schott, a 'kor' corresponds to about 250 quarts, so these horns would have stored 375 gallons of oil.)

So far nobody has thought about the information given in this clear and factual manner: 'bull's horns' contain large quantities of oil. Therefore:

> This was definitely not a wild bull (a fact which is repeatedly emphasized in the epic), but a fighting machine whose 'snortings' would cast up large holes in which the men of Uruk became engulfed (Gilgamesh Epic, tablet VI, pp.125-130), while the supposed horns were most likely its oil sumps or petrol tanks.

In that case the figures given would be correct, for they correspond to the fuel capacity of a large tank. It would also explain why Gilgamesh handed over these horns to the

108

armourers, the technicians of the town of Uruk: he meant to sacrifice the oil to his tutelary god Lugalbanda. No wonder that subsequently (as it says in lines 176/7) he and Enkidu had to wash their hands in the Euphrates.

However, Gilgamesh and Enkidu come across this oil yet again; in S. Kramer's version of the myth (which has been translated from cuneiform texts), it says that Gilgamesh once lost some magic tools which dropped into the 'underworld'. His friend Enkidu volunteered to recover them and received this warning from Gilgamesh: he must not wear 'clean clothing' and, above all, he must not 'spill any of the good oil of the vehicle', for those who lived in the underworld would smell it. It would seem that they were not very partial to the oil of the gods.

The oil is not seen to be endowed with any mystical characteristics, but is the oil used in a vehicle. Furthermore, there seem to have been several kinds, each with a different smell, just as today an expert could tell which petrol and oil a car uses by their smells.

What remains obscure is the identity of the 'underworld': was this another planet, or the 'underground' of those prehistoric Tupamaros, the Titans and Asurs, deadly enemies of the gods here on Earth? This would explain why Enkidu was to wear no 'clean clothing' during his journey into their realm. A man would stand out like a sore thumb if he were to mix with guerillas dressed in dinner-jacket or tails, for example, especially if he had that typically upper-class smell about him—and it would seem that with the gods smell was the smell of the fuel of their vehicles. (In 1945 it was possible to distinguish Americans, Frenchmen and Russians merely by the smell of their cigarettes.)

What is clear is that the oil came from the gods and was therefore sacred; they refuelled their spaceships with it before they started for heaven, which is why their memorials and statues were later anointed with it.

And because of this misunderstood tradition a dying man is even today supplied with oil by his priest—for a smooth flight into the next world.

Should he recover, however, the Church will ascribe this to the healing effect of the oily sacrament. There are archetypal examples for this too: the oil (or fuel) of the gods' vehicles and flying craft has always been regarded as the 'water of life', possessing healing powers. Doubtless this is a mistake, for the life-force referred to the gods' vehicles, which occasionally had to drink a 'drink of life' (=a refuel), like the Garuda, mythical vehicle of the Indian god Vishnu.[56] It does not refer to either gods or men.

In Chinese tradition[57] the goddess Hsi-Wang-Mu guards the 'red water' at the foot of Mount K'unlun; all travellers had to drink some before embarking on a space journey. This too was probably a mix-up, for it was definitely not the passenger who drank it: it flowed into the tanks (the horns) of the gods' flying craft.

But since the gods apparently stayed eternally young (due to their regular replacement), their vehicles' 'drink of life' came to be equated with the 'water of life'.

Fuel, spirit and oil became healing medicines and have remained so to this very day. If this whole oil business were the only reference to the mainly technological background of the Christian religion and its rites, one might possibly entertain doubts, but as we have already seen, there exist any number of such connections and chains of causality.

In how many Sunday sermons, for example, is Christ's allged saying 'Knock, and it shall be opened unto you' (Matt. 7:7) quoted! This refers to the gate of heaven which, seven verses later (Matt. 7:13-14), is described as 'strait and narrow'. Perhaps today's preachers see this as only a poetic analogy. But the gate to be knocked upon was once a real door leading to the gods' installations and vehicles and which reacted to acoustic signals: the famous 'Open, Sesame!'.

In the Gilgamesh Epic Enkidu comes to a door 'to which he speaks as to a man'. The door, however, is 'unreasonable', and Enkidu cries in frustration that he would have 'brought an axe' if he had known what to expect. He says to it: 'Either, may any king who comes after me *awaken* you!...' (a clear reference to the programming code) 'or...'. After

110

that there is a gap in the cuneiform text, but Enkidu probably tore out the recalcitrant door and tossed it aside.

This is the first reference to a door which must be spoken to in order to open it.

Somehow this later strayed into the story of Jesus of Nazareth, in the same way that the story of the flood in the Gilgamesh Epic appears in the Old Testament, down to the smallest detail. Gilgamesh learns that Utnapishtim has built an 'ark', a box 60 yards long, and loaded it with animals and men (as well as gold and beer!) in order to escape a great flood. He landed on Mount Nissir and sent out a dove, then a swallow and then a raven. Only the raven failed to return.

All these arks might be recollections of the gods' methods of transport. Thus the Greek god Dionysus was washed up on the shore in a 'box'[58] together with his mother Semele (she, however, was dead by the time they came ashore). The 'birds' were remote-control reconnaissance probes, especially since boxes of certain types have always been held as sacred, having brought the gods to Earth and out of the sea.

In many Egyptian temples there are such boxes which stood on a 'ship' (!) and were carried about on special feast-days. [59]

> *The holy shrines of all periods—even Christian shrines containing the Holy of Holies—were fundamentally copies of containers of the gods, in which some of them were lowered to Earth from their ships. Our explorers land on the moon in the same way from an orbiting spaceship.*

The principles of space travel and landing techniques have always been the same and there is no reason why they should have been different then. Accidents did happen, as we have seen when Semele did not survive the landing.

We cannot assume that the gods had come to visit Earth only *once*. It is probable that our planet had visitors from space many times and at varying intervals. As recently as November 1972 a tremendous sensation was created when the British scientist Richard Leaky discovered the bones of a

111

man who lived two and a half million years ago near Lake Rudolph in Kenya. This is more than a million years older than the previous oldest man, Australopithecus. Moreover, the Kenya man is not nearly as ape-like as Australopithecus; on the contrary, he bears a remarkable resemblance to us.

Not only has a part of the theory of evolution thus been thrown into doubt, but also those beautiful theories about the naked ape who climbed down from a tree. Kenya man was certainly no tree-dweller. Where did he come from and where did he go?

This sudden localized appearance of higher forms of human life, existing as they did for a time alongside quite primitive ones, only partly to disappear again, leads us to believe that the strangers came many times, leaving behind physical proof of their presence.

The last great wave of divine visitors seems to have been one of several. We shall have to learn to think in cosmic terms, using criteria that are different from those we have used so far. This applies to ourselves as well as to our religions. The age of narrow outlook and of miracles has come to an end; the time has come for the age of science to begin.

5 In the footsteps of the immortals

In order to prove the impotence of their gods and to convert the Germans to the Christian faith, Saint Boniface (his German name was Winfrith) is said to have felled an oak tree consecrated to Thor.

We of the 20th century cannot get away so easily; to break the domination of millenia-old conceptions of magic we will have to remove whole forests of taboos, with not even a paradise in store by way of reward, such as Boniface promised the Germans.

However, there is one consolation. His paradise from which Adam and Eve were supposedly driven and the prospect of which Jesus held out to one of the malefactors who were being executed together with him on the cross (Luke 23:43: 'Today thou shalt be with me in paradise')— this paradise, then, is no other-worldly holiday resort, but was originally a concept of something quite real, both for the prohibited areas of the gods on Earth and for the cosmic worlds that were their homes.

The word paradise comes from Old Persian *pardéz— pairi-daéza*, meaning something like 'enclosure' or 'garden', i.e. a fenced-in area. According to the report in the Old Testament, the first men bred by the gods were allowed to live in such a zoological-botanical garden until they hit upon the idea of raiding a 'tree'. It is reasonable to suppose that 'divine trees' in almost all of man's legends may be equated with rocket-shaped spacecraft belonging to the gods. Such vehicles would have been parked also in the biblical 'garden of Eden'. They were, of course, strictly prohibited to human assistants. Whether it was a serpent (a Titan?) who tempted them to sidle up to such an object 'in order to become like the gods' ('eritis sicut dii'), or whether that was only an excuse after they had been found out, is impossible to say. At any rate, their punishment was that they were turned out of 'pardéz'.

Modern theologians and painstaking philosophers have claimed that this is a parable of man's awakening from the innocence of animal existence to self-consciousness and bitter self-knowledge. But we cannot assume that men had developed such theories tens of thousands of years ago. Besides, it is very odd that almighty God-Father (as we read in Genesis 3:9) went to look for Adam who had hidden himself, calling, 'Where *art* thou?' only to throw him and his wife out later, accompanied by wild curses.

Rather this brings to mind a picture of a surly and infuriated captain who has caught some earthly half-men red-handed, trying to break in. His reaction is logical and pragmatic, in that he places 'Cherubims, and a flaming sword which turned every way' (Gen. 3:24) at the entrance to paradise—i.e. mechanical robot guardians. No Creator would have had to use 'flaming swords' against naked natives!

In addition to this earthly paradise there are other legendary paradises on other heavenly bodies. For the Toltecs this paradise was the home of Quetzalcoatl, a world lit by a gently equable light.[1] The Chugash in Alaska[2] and the Micronesians of the South Seas[3] believed in a similar paradise.

None of these paradises—and this surely is the essential point—is described as in any way supernatural or otherworldly. Basically they are very earthly, only perhaps more beautiful and comfortable. Details such as directions, distances, size, style of buildings, etc., are supplied, and all without the fantastic exaggeration one might expect in a fairy-tale or poetic invention.

For these paradises are no fairy-tale. Their depiction is based on descriptions by beings who had come to Earth from them. What is interesting is the constantly recurring mention of 'mild and diffused light' in contrast to that on Earth.

From this information one may deduce that there were different atmospheric conditions on these worlds. And yet how could people in Alaska, South America and the South Seas have arrived at practically identical conceptions, had they not received them from the same source—the gods?

Understandably they were homesick, and when the last of them were unable to return home (for reasons so far unknown) they passed on their longing for paradise to their successors and descendants here on Earth—including Christ and including us.

But Christianity is not the only religion and doctrine almost entirely based on this and other of the gods' traditions. Most religions have roots in them to a greater or lesser degree.

Indian Brahmanism and Hinduism are based on the written recordings of the old myths—the Rig-Veda (=knowledge) and the Bhagavadgitâ. The Rig-Veda (six times the size of the Bible) was first recorded in about 1500 BC; the Bhagavadgitâ, with its 700-plus verses, a little later.[4]

Both 'bibles' and both forms of religion are distinguished by a vast number of deities and godlike earthly heroes. They all perform miracles incessantly (a rich store for anybody following in the tracks of the cosmic gods and their knowledge). Naturally, at least the major gods of these religions came from heaven (called the 'avâtara', the Descent of Krishna and of other gods); they used 'vimanas', fiery flying vehicles and magic weapons, which are described in every technical detail. One report[5] says that when the god Rama was threatened by an 'army of monkeys' (men or robots?) he put a 'magic arrow' into action. This produces a flash of lightning 'stronger than the heat from a hundred thousand suns', turning everything into dust. The hair of survivors falls out, their nails disintegrate.

We know of such magic weapons from Sodom and Gomorrha, and from Hiroshima and Nagasaki.

Even here we find miracles everywhere, while far in the background rules Brahma or Ishvara, the intrinsic archetypal god,[6] similar to that of Christianity.

Here too the external effect of the gods has usurped most

115

of the real knowledge of the great overall truths[7] that they brought to us.

In this confusion of technically-conditioned 'faith', the teaching of Gautama Buddha seems to stand all by itself:

Buddha lived between about 560 and 480 BC.[8] Son of a Sakya prince, he was born in Kapilavastu in Nepal at the foot of the Himalayas. Till he was twenty-nine he lived in wealth and luxury (as did Mohammed at a later date). He had a wife, and a son called Rahula. Then he suddenly decided to become a simple itinerant monk, and he left wife, child and palace without farewell. After years of restless wandering and disappointment he received inspiration by the river Neranyara under a fig tree (the 'tree of knowledge'). From then until his death in about his eightieth year he proclaimed his teaching, which at first glance seems to be totally different from all others so far considered.

For it does not rely on the gods, but solely on man and his soul, which is to be redeemed from the cycle of rebirths so that, through his own will, it is ultimately absorbed in 'nirvâna'. ('Nirvâna' is generally and mistakenly equated with 'nothing'; it is rather the concept of 'non-self', the oneness with and participation in a superior being.)

Buddha's original teaching contained no heaven, no hell, no paradise and no personified god, but only the goal of redemption from the entanglement of the laws of causality (the 'karma')—and it endeavours to show the way.

It is not known who Buddha really was (his second family name was Gautama and his 'baptismal' name Siddharta). The fact of his earthly existence does, however, appear to be a little better documented than that of Jesus of Nazareth; in 1898, in a 'stupa' (a small, stone-built, bell-shaped temple) near Piprava in India, were discovered remains of ashes as well as a document written in Brahmanee, which identified them as his remains—Buddha having been cremated after his death.[9]

The earliest pictorial representations of Gautama Buddha come from the province of Gandhara in Afghanistan, where he is said to have lived and worked; they display typically European-Greek features in face as well as in clothing.

Gandhara was one of the areas which became independent principalities and kingdoms after the death of Alexander the Great (323 BC); the possibility of Buddha's Greek-occidental origin cannot therefore be altogether dismissed.

Both his way of thinking as well as his world of thought are in fact more closely related to the Greek philosophers than to other religions' fantasies about gods; his state of non-self, the nirvâna, corresponds more to the presumable (intrinsic) reality of being—even according to the knowledge of modern mathematics and physics, and, as it were, confirmed by it—than to the paradise and heaven of the usual folk mythologies.

One might term the teaching of Buddha the first psychological-parapsychological doctrine: it is more of a science than a religion.

Yet, although Buddha did not think very highly of the gods (he acknowledged them, but anthropophuistically thought that they too were mortal), he unintentionally adopted essential areas of their tradition; the teaching of reincarnation—according to which a man has to be reborn until all his deeds (his karma) have been balanced—existed long before Buddha in Indian Brahmanism and in the Tibetan Bon religion. This latter religion has very close connections with the gods. The Bon-po (followers of the Bon doctrine) tell of seven divine kings who had descended from heaven on a rope (!) and returned in the same way. An eighth king remained on Earth for ever—because he had been murdered by his earthly ministers.[10]

This might be regarded as at least *one* aspect of the origin of the incarnation doctrine: the gods, or god-kings, came and went, and came back again. In the eyes of the mortals they died and were reborn, and only when they had completed their service here on Earth were they allowed to stay at home in heaven. It would appear in this respect that 'transfer to the stars', popular in later Greek mythology, must be taken almost literally. Apart from this, history shows clearly that the gods were certainly physically mortal, not phantom beings. According to earthly conceptions of time they gained real or supposed immortality chiefly by technical means. The

117

Bon-po, incidentally,[11] originated the idea that after his departure from Earth a man must spend forty-nine days in a kind of limbo until he is either reborn or finally released from service on Earth.

From this came the well known Bardo Thödol, the Tibetan Book of the Dead.[12] It contains precise directions as to the thought impulses and advice which priests and bereaved must send after the deceased during these forty-nine days in order to guide him safely through all dangers of his half-beyond existence.

Once again the comparison with a control station for astronauts occurs to anyone who has read even only a few extracts of the Bardo Thödol, or who has heard the chanted instructions of lama priests: they too are in continuous radio-telephone contact with the passengers in the spacecraft, giving them advice.

> Modern astronauts fly through space as we know it; the gods, during their zero-time flights and physical space-walks, flew or walked in part through different physical states of being. Doubtless they required instructions from a control base.

Could the instructions of the Bardo be a recollection of this? Basically the stories and legends of Christ's descent into hell are nothing more than remembrances of divine flights and walks into the 'beyond'.

One question remains: What was the purpose of all this? Why did they step into the sepulchres and transformation chambers? The answer is that apparently they were doing what has been described quite clearly in many legends and traditions—they 'bowed' the heavens (Psalms 144:5). They moved the Earth from its place, as told by Vishnu in the Varâna Purana[13] and elsewhere. In brief they worked, so to speak, as cosmic fitters. How they did this may be surmised in a bold, retrospective science-fiction scene, which is admittedly based on analogous laws and conclusions in physics:

Let us assume that a god has semi-materially transformed

himself in a 'furnace' chamber in the manner already mentioned. He then ascends and floats between dimensions in a somewhat unstable state, rather like plasma of a higher order; part dependent on, part independent of, time and space. By will-power he would be able to increase his half-existing 'body' until planets and suns shrank in comparison to the size of footballs. Then he could play with them.

This has often been ascribed to the gods but not understood so far. It is a risky game, for any change in the extremely unstable balance of energy might immediately turn him into a man with nothing but body which would either perish from the heat of the sun or freeze in the coldness of space.

His state would be anything but exalted or wonderful. Proportions would continually change as in a distorting mirror; now he would feel himself to be as small as an atom, now large enough to handle the orbit of several planets.

How was he to 'move' planets or suns? With his 'hand'? We shall have to equip our astro-fitter with a tool, and in fact such an object seems to have existed. It was some kind of ladle, hook or scythe—according to our local earthly conceptions, that is. Of course, during a transformation it would have changed with the astro-fitter, just as tools of our moon explorers have a different weight on the moon.

With this tool, our trail becomes tangible and concrete again. It turns up in traditions all over the world. In the Varâna Purana, Vishnu 'lifts' the Earth into the sunlight with the aid of a 'boar's tooth'; with the Polynesians[14] the same work is carried out with a 'fishing hook'; in Greek legend, the archetypal god Uranus busies himself in the sky with a 'stone scythe'; and among the ancient Tibetan Bon-po[15] the god of wisdom, Shen-Iha-od-dkar, directs heavenly bodies with an 'iron hook'.

This tool is often equated with the hands or fingers of the gods: in the Egyptian Book of the Dead,[16] the deity's fingers and toes are likened to serpents; and the figure of a goddess from 1st century BC Greece has her right arm changed into a 'pirate's hook'.

From prehistory onwards we find the custom of 'finger sacrifice' among many different peoples. When a headman (i.e. God) died, his relations chopped off one of his fingers, or at least a joint. There are impressions of hands mutilated in this manner in the stone-age caves of Altamira, Gargas, Les Cabarets, etc. But more interesting still is the cave of El Castillo near Punte Viesgo in Spain; groups of red dots have been arranged round colour impressions of partly mutilated hands.[1][7] Are these perhaps meant to represent (manipulated) heavenly bodies?

Every superstition has its root in reality, and thus we may conclude that these are distorted echoes of the gods' work, of their cosmic activities, when they may have burnt not only their tools—the hooks, teeth, scythes, etc.—but literally also their fingers. And this was dutifully emulated by the natives of Earth who cut off their own fingers and joints.

The scythe and the hook turn up in earthly (and originally mystical-sacred) 'games' as 'sacred tools'; for example, that game of hockey played in Ethiopia thousands of years ago, and the South American 'Pelota' where the players also use hook-shaped rackets. The Aztecs used shuttlecocks in another sacred game, which was a matter of life and death for the players.

Games, then, were played in imitation of the sometimes lethal games played by the gods, for whom it was not a matter of balls or shuttlecocks, but of stars and solar systems.

This explains at last why the gods submitted to procedures as complex as the 'transformation': not to impress native earthmen, but in order to carry out assignments apparently set within the framework of cosmic order.

According to Toltec legend (see page 1) Nanahuatzin and his divine colleague Teccuciztecatl undertook one of the most dangerous tasks ever, even for beings as technically experienced as the gods. Although there are frequent reports of such ascensions to heaven, there are scarcely any about people coming back: 'Ascension commandos' in the true sense of the word. As mentioned before, this must remain, for the time being at least, as some sort of past Utopia, or a theory, but it is one that is conceivable and feasible according to the laws of theoretical physics![8] However, it was not theory under any circumstances at the time, nor something

120

to do with a magically supernatural lift-off into a fantasy heaven.

It was no theory, in the same way that the gods' stepping through a zero-time transmission appliance (i.e. a 'gate') did not mean their transfer to a 'beyond' in any religious sense, but rather a high-speed transport from one point in the Universe to another. In the science and technology of the day after tomorrow that, too, will seem quite natural to us.

> *To repeat: There was nothing miraculous, enigmatic or magical about the gods. In the last analysis, everything they did was 'natural'; sorcery, magic and religions result solely from either lack of understanding or misinterpretation on the part of human beings.*

It was because people watched the gods disappearing into their machines, full of youth and vigour, and then watched them reappear unchanged, that the idea of *physical* existence after death occurred to them at all.

It was probably because people saw the gods take provisions on board for their space journeys (when they were using space craft), that they too put food and tools in the graves of their dead.

How else could people, observing that corpses rot and disintegrate, have hit upon the idea that bodies might live on and possibly even require food? How would it have been possible for people to talk and dream of paradise (and also of evil and unfriendly worlds) unless someone had described such places to them or perhaps even taken them there?

Finally, how could reports of the gods' strange hook- or scythe-shaped tools have originated (and that invariably in connection with cosmic manipulations), unless such objects had actually existed sometime, somewhere, somehow, and unless people had discovered how they were used?

Resurrection . . . the next world . . . paradise . . . life eternal: all this was once reality, otherwise we should never have received information about it; even if it were only a question of longing or wishing for a thing, one would still, at some stage, have had to have formed a conception of it in one's

121

mind. Nothing (as the bard has it) will come of nothing.

We do not know whether the gods had a religion of their own since nothing has been recorded. There remains thus only one theory: *the gods themselves had neither gods nor religion.* Even if they did, it could only have been a doctrine on the lines of Buddha's teachings, never a religion of pseudo-realities.

Why should it be necessary for the gods to believe what they knew to be a fact? They knew about the possibility of modifications of time and space. They could (at least in part) transform themselves. Compared to Earth dwellers they lived longer, if not for ever. They were presumably familiar with dimensions and planes different from those to which we are accustomed. They mastered forces which we dare approach only slowly and with trepidation.[19]

The hierarchical structure of their world, then, looked something like this:

At the top was the 'god of the worlds', the master of the Universe—Brahma, Anu, etc. Below him were the system or star gods (Sin, Shamash in the Gilgamesh Epic). They were followed by the planet gods and gods of land, one of whom was Jehovah. Their assistants were the angels (=messengers). Then came demigods, like Heracles, Quetzalcoatl, and Gilgamesh ('He is two parts god, his third part is man...', tablets 1,2). They were followed by corporeal, earthly man. Finally there were the Titans, Asurs, Giants and whatever else they were called, isolated and hostile, hierarchically equal to planet and land gods.

This is not an invented order, and neither are they invented 'spirit beings'. This was the cosmic order as it existed then, and these were the entities and intelligences that existed in that cosmic order. At most it was the names given them by men that were invented, and they were probably names or designations from the language of the gods.

Any African tribesman or South American Indian today will equate the name Nixon with that of the President of the USA, although they are not always identical. Accordingly, Anu, Vishnu, etc. were not unique phenomena, but functionaries of a certain structure, of a certain order in a certain system.

Now let us compare the Christian hierarchy with that of the gods:

At the top is God the Father, lord of all existence. Below him are the archangels in charge of the world. They are followed by the earth-related redeemer godhead Jesus—for the Egyptians this was Osiris. Approximately of equal status were the angels. Then come semi-deities, the host of saints and Mary, and finally once again corporeal man. Isolated and hostile are Satan and his entourage—the expelled archangel and light-bearer.

The structure of both hierarchies is the same; only the designations are different.

In principle this is the same in most religions:

> *The hierarchy of the existing gods was taken over and*
> *assumed different names—no better, no worse and no*
> *different from today when developing countries play at*
> *and emulate democracy without the least idea of its true*
> *nature.*

To a greater or lesser degree all world religions are such copies and adaptations. This may be proved geographically. The nearer the subsequent religious centres (e.g. in Egypt, Asia Minor, China and South America) were to the former 'residences' of the gods, the clearer and more distinct is their tradition; the further away they were, and the less frequently they had contact with the gods (e.g. in northern Europe and North America), the more obscure and unintelligible are their traditions.[20]

They wore crowns and tiaras of gold, encrusted with precious stones, and thought they were wearing the helmets of the gods; they clutched rods and thought they were holding the power of the gods; they built temples and castles, stone copies of the gods' technical installations, and thought they possessed the key to eternal life and to the next world: childish conceptions, considered scientifically and technologically, but they were the foundation of every power and religious system for ten thousand years. All we hold in our hands are fragments, splinters and pieces of what once was.

It is really only an accident that the miracle-making rabbi from Palestine strayed into the story and became the founder of a faith *malgré lui*.[2] [1]He no more ascended into heaven than you or I.

> *Today, when we stand beneath the Christmas tree celebrating the birth of Christ, we are really celebrating the arrival on Earth of an alien and distant god or demigod thousands of years ago. When at Easter we celebrate his entombment and resurrection, we are really remembering the transformation and ascension of some of our true ancestors. Perhaps they deserve to be remembered because they have helped our Earth—then again, perhaps they don't.*

Should we take this farewell to religion to heart, for it is in fact not just a question of the Christian religion only, but of all forms of religion which are predominantly based on ignorant emulation of the gods?

What benefits, after all, have we gained from religion? Illusions, superstition, magic—some good things and some bad. If we were to draw up a balance sheet, we might at best come out even: not exactly a great success. The successful ones, at any rate, were those who have always thrived on religion as a business.

The gigantic scope of this business was revealed and illustrated as recently as 1972 during the latest excavations of the British archaeologist W.B. Emery in Sakkara, the subterranean 'city of the dead' near Memphis in Egypt. There, a system of passages several floors high and extending over many miles was discovered. They were (and still are) crammed with *hundreds and thousands* of ibis, falcons and baboons embalmed in clay tubes—offerings by pious Egyptian petitioners to the gods, whose sacred animals these were supposed to be. These donations were churned out commercially (often the bones did not match) and sold. There must have been regular animal-breeding farms for this particular trade; the main profit, needless to say, was made by the priests.

One can make comparisons with similar Christian customs in Europe and elsewhere.

The business side is the least objectionable aspect of man's adoption of 'divine' traditions. Uglier and more gory is the long trail of men, women and children, senselessly butchered for religious reasons, and in this respect the successors to the so-called herald of humanity and pity have established an unenviable record.

Measured by the number of inhabitants of the continent at that time, the five to six *million* (eight or nine, according to other estimates) heretics and witches sent to the stake or the block[22] in Europe alone represent a figure far in excess of what even the most bloodthirsty idols of Babylon, Carthage and the Aztecs demanded by way of tribute.

Not included in this figure are those murdered in other countries and continents, and all those who died in so-called religious wars 'for the cross'. Of the innumerable descriptions available, one only shall serve to illustrate the way in which the 'Christianization' of a country like Mexico was carried out. It is taken from the 'Codex Florentino' which was written around 1585, and the original of which is at Nahuatl.[23]

The Aztecs had planned to celebrate the feast of their god Huitzilopochtli, and the Spaniards, who had arrived in the country shortly before, wanted to participate in the festivities. At this feast the bravest warriors and chieftains performed a ritual dance in the temple courtyard.

But suddenly the watching Spaniards were seized by an overwhelming blood-lust. They barred every exit and attacked the dancers. The following is a literal extract from the report: 'Then they attacked the dancers, stabbing them to death, running them through with their lances, killing them with their swords. . . . They ripped out the arms of some, slit open the bellies of others so that their entrails poured out onto the ground. Some tried to run away, but their entrails dragged in front of them and their feet got entangled in them . . . they could not escape. . . . The blood of chieftains flowed like water and collected in puddles.' This took place Anno Domini 1521—in the name of the Father and the Son and the Holy Ghost; and in the name of the True Church, in which alone salvation is to be found.

'That was long ago, that's how people were in those days, and today the Church is quite different . . .' say the objectors. But in reply one might say this: Pope Paul VI has done nothing to help check the population explosion, though like any thinking person he must know that sooner or later it will lead to famine and mutual destruction of millions of people. Although he could contribute significantly towards the solution of this problem, he does nothing. Such a Pope and such a Church are indirectly guilty of causing this millionfold misery, and are in no way different from those members of Dutch sects who prefer to let their children die rather than allow them to be inoculated or operated on, merely because they have drawn wrong conclusions from certain ancient tomes of misinterpretation. There is yet another argument to be refuted, one which is usually proffered with great alacrity: the fact that Christianity has been able to last for two thousand years is 'proof of its sanctity and God-ordainedness', irrespective of whether Jesus was more or less a mortal man. This assertion is utter mockery; the opposite is correct:

> Christianity has lasted so long, not because it was or is 'divinely inspired', but solely because it usurped for its own purposes the dread and reverence which had been indelibly implanted and programmed in the minds of Earth dwellers by the real and human gods, and because it took over the traditions of those gods.
>
> The vestments of the Christian Church were borrowed; they have become threadbare and are slowly disintegrating.

In this context it is irrelevant that a Jesuit father like Paolo de Gall believes himself able to prove that the alleged grave-cloth of Christ is genuine.[24] Even if it were so, it at best amounts to no more than that this portentous cloth may have covered the face or body of a man who was executed on the cross. Perhaps it was the historic rabbi Jeshu, perhaps not. However, the cloth in no way signifies either that he rose or that he was the Son of God.

It will no longer be possible to save the dying Church even with the paraphernalia of grave-cloths (of which there are several), splinters and nails from the alleged cross of Christ, or bones of saints and martyrs.

Priests and believers leave the Church in droves. In tiny Austria alone the number of people leaving the Church has doubled since 1958 (it was more than 21,000 in 1970). While in November 1972, in an open letter to the Pope, the former professor and vice-dean of the faculty of theology at the University of Vienna, Professor Dr Hubertus Mynarek, declared his refusal to serve him any longer, and accused him of lust for power and absolutism.

At the same time, all over the world sects dispensing magic and humbug flourish to their hearts' content. In less than two years the fourteen-year-old (!) Indian 'god' Maharaj Ji, in his 'Mission of the Divine Light', managed to gather six million followers, mainly in America. (That at the end of 1972 he was caught smuggling diamonds in England does not bother them.) On the other hand, this is no ground either for ecclesiastic-Christian jubilation, for this youth draws the crowds not because, as Pope Paul VI in 1972 mused so profoundly, 'the smoke of Satan is invading the edifice of the Church', but because these Churches are failing. Or, put more plainly, because they are losing their footing; a footing which was never genuine, but artificial from the very beginning.

But what about latter-day miracles, like those miraculous cures at Lourdes and elsewhere; appearances of Mary; stigmatizations; or the late father Pio's 'levitation', witnessed by many people in Italy? Could they not be regarded as proof of (or allusion to) the power and might of the Christian religion? For believers, unfortunately not. Every one of these manifestations proves no more than the existence of man's parapsychological, para-normal abilities and of corresponding energies outside his corporeity. And these were in existence long before Christianity.

The Russians and the Americans are carrying out intensive research into the nature of these forces, which are as real and effective as any forces of 'normal' physics and which are known by the collective name of psi. In his book *The psychic Long-range Effect* (Moscow 1962), the Soviet doyen of this science, Professor Leonid L. Vasilyev, stated that 'the establishment of such energies' was 'equal to the liberation of intra-atomic energy'; the American Professor J.B. Rhine arrived at similar conclusions. [25]

The effect of spiritual forces and conceptions on, say, physical processes has been known to medicine for some considerable time. If a doctor treats a wart on a child's finger with water, telling him that it will be gone in a day, it is likely to do so. This is the result of a psi force, called the 'placebo' effect in medical circles (from the Latin *placebo*, 'I shall be pleasing' or 'acceptable'). It is quite feasible that even a cancerous swelling may dissolve almost spontaneously if the concentrated psi energy of the patient, as well as of the people around him (being in a state of religious ecstasy), exerts an influence on it. That this does not always happen may be due to man's lack of ability to control these forces; after all, not everyone is a thought-reader or a clairvoyant, although the existence of people with these abilities is incontestable. In consequence, a more or less fortuitous success is regarded as 'grace'. Levitation is a similar example. It is said that in his religious ecstasy St Joseph of Copertino floated 'almost thirty yards towards the altar'. [26] Levitation is regarded as neither swindle nor miracle, for modern physics states that the force of gravity is probably based on a still unknown wave motion which could therefore readily be superimposed and neutralized by a 'higher' form of energy; presumably man may be able to produce this energy himself in exceptional circumstances, but it might also be possible to produce it by technological means.

The neutralization of the force of gravity is one of the gods' major secrets. From all the information recorded in legends they seem to have mastered it, either technologically or by way of a physical source of energy of their own. It is not the task of this book to describe and explore the

128

phenomena of psi forces in detail. In this context they are of interest only in so far as they may be regarded as existing according to the most recent discoveries of science; and also in so far as they offer a logical and reasonable explanation for all the above-mentioned miracles of faith.

For instance, science is aware that it is particularly children in puberty who may involuntarily release unusual psi forces[27] (many a ghost or poltergeist is explained in this way); if a powerful religious imagination is added to this—as with the children who saw apparitions of Mary at Lourdes and Fatima—this energy will clearly show itself in the figure of Our Lady in their minds. These and other believers invariably saw the Holy Virgin in exactly the form in which she was familiar and known to them.

> *To have carried on religious propaganda with the aid of what are after all the products of people's own imagination is not exactly to the credit of Church history or politics. Tomorrow all these phenomena and problems will belong within the scope of an unprejudiced and dispassionate science.*

The disenchantment with our previous conception of the world is a disagreeable and painful process for many people, but it has become inexorable today. Thousands of years of artificially nurtured and maintained superstition are real enough. This is the great context in which we must see things: Our world, a planet like millions of others in the Universe, was in close contact with others of this Universe, with sister planets and brother men, for many millions of years. The last appearance of the gods is in this context only *one* episode, as is the last ice age seen in the context of Earth's history. The cosmic gods who last landed here left behind a wealth of seemingly obscure knowledge which degenerated into religions and superstitions.

This episode has now ended. Some form of programming—possibly inherited from the gods or stored in our brains by them—has begun to awaken and vigorously to herald a new era.

129

Why it does so at this precise moment, we do not know.

All at once we are flung into the loneliness and cold of the cosmos, more naked and bare than ever a Jesus could have been when he cried out for his *abba* ('father'). This is not our fault; it is the inheritance of millenia of development gambled and embezzled away, of a development which might have been.

One hope remains: that we may succeed in re-establishing the spiritual connection with the time when the true and real tradition of the gods ceased and the great darkness of the spirit began; that we may find again the trail and the path of the immortals in time and eternity.

The ancient Germanic Edda laments:

> 'Walgrind is the barred gate
> standing on the ground
> sacred before sacred doors;
> old is the barred gate,
> yet few forebode
> how its lock is locked. . . .'

We must find the key. It is our only chance.

References

Chapter 1.

1. A. Posnansky, *Tiahuanaco*, New York, n.e., 1945.
2. W. Bennett, *Ancient Arts of the Andes*, New York, 1966.
3. Hyatt A. Verrill, *American Ancient Civilizations*, New York, 1953; London, 1954.
4. A.E. Jensen, *Myth and Cult Among Primitive Peoples*, Chicago, 1963.
5. Johannes Leipoldt, *Sterbende und auferstehende Götter*, Leipzig, 1923.
6. Joseph Klausner, *From Jesus to Paul*, London, 1946.
7. J.B. Rhine, *The Reach of the Mind*, London, 1948.
8. Kurt Frischler, *Geisterstunde der Gelehrten*, Munich, 1971.
9. W. Krickeberg *et al.*, *Pre-Columbian American Religions*, London, 1968.
10. Wolfgang Schadewaldt, *Griechische Sternsagen*, Munich, 1970.
11. Karl F. Kohlenberg, *Enträtselte Vorzeit*, Munich, 1970.
12. Julius Schwabe, *Archetyp und Tierkreis*, Basle, 1951.
13. Erich Zehren, *Der gehenkte Gott*, Berlin, 1959.
14. Josef Menzel, *Das Erbe der Ahnen*, Prague, 1935.
15. R. Mühleisen, 'Der Kugelblitz, ein Plasmazustand?', in *Kosmos*, April 1972.
16. Hermann Rasche, *Das Christusmysterium*, Bremen, 1954.
17. Josef Leo Seifert, *Die Sinnbedeutung des Mythos*, Vienna, 1954.
18. P. Grimal, *Larousse World Mythology*, vol. 3, Feltham, 1969.
19. G.G. Scholem, *Major Trends in Jewish Mysticism*, London, 1955; New York, 1961.
20. Carl Schneider, *Geistesgeschichte des antiken Christentums*, Munich, 1954.
21. as 11.
22 Robert Charroux, *Les Maîtres du Monde*, Paris, 1971.

Chapter 2.

1. Müller/Kuales, 'Die Goten', in H. Reinerth, *Vorgeschichte der deutschen Stämme*, 1940.
2. E. Dammann, *Die Religionen Afrikas*, Stuttgart, 1963.
3. A. Heidel, *The Babylonian Genesis*, Chicago, 1942.
4. W.G. Lambert *et al.*, *Atra-Hasis, The Babylonian Story of the Flood*, Oxford, 1969.
5. A. Braghine, *The Shadow of Atlantis*, London, 1938.
6. Karl F. Kohlenberg, *op. cit.*
7. Hoimar von Ditfurth, *Kinder des Weltalls*, Hamburg, 1970.
8. J. Cerney, *Ancient Egyptian Religion*, London, 1952.
9. as 2.
10. E. Peterich, *Götter und Helden der Germanen*, Olten, 1955.
11. H.C. Puech, *Le Manichéisme, son fondateur, sa doctrine*, Paris, 1949.
12. F. Creuzer, *Symbolik und Mythologie der alten Völker*, Leipzig/Darmstadt, 1919.
13. W. Pferdekamp, *Die Indianderstory*, Munich, 1963.
14. J. Legge, *The Shoo King*, contained in 'The Chinese Classics', Hong Kong/Oxford, 1961.
15. A. Reisenfeld, *The Megalithic Culture of Melanesia*, Leiden, 1950.
16. W. Cordan, *Das Buch des Rates—Popol Vuh*, Düsseldorf, 1962.
17. W. Schneider, *Babylon Is Everywhere*, London, 1963.
18. S.N. Kramer, *Sumerian Mythology*, Philadelphia, 1944.
19. W. Vollmer, *Wörterbuch der Mythologie aller Völker*, Stuttgart, 1859.
20. as 6.
21. Will Durant, *Life of Greece*, London and New York, 1939.
22. F. Genzmer, *Die Edda*, Jena, 1934/1938.

23. Aeschylus, *Prometheus Bound*.
24. Eduard Meyer, *Ursprung und Anfänge des Christentums*, Stuttgart/Berlin, 1921/1924.
25. E. Lönnrot, *Kalevala*, Cambridge, Mass., 1963.
26. R.H.W. Empson, *The Cult of the Peacock Angel*, London, 1928.
27. W. Seabrook, *Adventure in Arabia*, London, 1931.
28. as 22.
29. Otto H. Muck, *Atlantis gefunden?*, Stuttgart, 1954.
30. Leo Frobenius, *Kulturgeschichte Afrikas*, Frankfurt, 1933.
31. as 17.
32. P. Raingeard, *Hermes Psychagogué*, Paris, 1965.
33. Herodotus, *Histories*.
34. Mircia Eliade, *Myth of Eternal Return*, London and Princeton, USA, 1954.
35. Georg Baesecke, *Vorgeschichte des Deutschen Schrifttums*, Halle/Saale, 1940.
36. Josef Leo Seifert, *op. cit.*
37. Will Durant, *Our Oriental Heritage*, London and New York, 1935.
38. Max Ebert, *Reallexikon der Vorgeschichte*, Berlin, 1924/1932.
39. Franz König, *Christus und die Religionen der Erde*, Vienna/Freiburg, 1951.
40. Alfred Jeremias, *Handbuch der altorientalischen Geisteskultur*, Berlin/Leipzig, 1929.
41. Apollodorus, *Works*.
42. A. Schott, *Das Gilgamesch-Epos*, Stuttgart, 1958.
43. Oswald Menghin, *Weltgeschichte der Steinzeit*, Vienna, 1940.
44. Hans Weinert, *Der geistige Aufstieg der Menschheit*, Stuttgart, 1951.
45. Carl Schuchhardt, *Alteuropa, die Entwicklung seiner Kulturen und Völker*, Berlin, 1941.
46. Joel Carmichael, *Death of Jesus*, London, 1963.
47. Johannes Lehmann, *The Jesus Report*, London, 1972.

Chapter 3.

1. Gerhard Strube, *Wer war Jesus von Nazareth*, Munich, 1872.
2. Flavius Josephus.
3. Erich Zehren, *op. cit.*
4. Joseph Klausner, *op.cit.*
5. Carl Schneider, *op. cit.*
6. A. Baur, *Apollonius von Tyana und Christus*, 1832.
7. Will Durant, *Caesar and Christ*, London and New York, 1944.
8. W. Bousset, *Kyrios Christos*, Göttingen, 1965.
9. O. Weinreich, *Antike Heilswunder*, 1909.
10. Wilhelm Schmidt, *Bibel im Kreuzverhör*, Gütersloh, 1968.
11. Adolf Jülicher, *Einleitung in das Neue Testament*, Tübingen, 1931.
12. Jean Schorer, *Pourquoi je suis devenu un chrétien libéral*, Geneva, 1971.
13. Eduard Meyer, *op. cit.*
14. Albert Schott, *op. cit.*
15. Margarete Riemenschneider, *Augengott und Heilige Hochzeit*, Leipzig, 1953.
16. H. Schrade, *Götter und Menschen Homers*, Stuttgart, 1952.
17. Kurt Lange, *König Echnaton und die Anarnazeit*, Munich, 1951.
18. Wolfgang Schadewaldt, *op. cit.*
19. Homer, *Odyssey*.
20. E. Dammann, *op. cit.*
21. P. Grimal, *op. cit.*
22. as 18.
23. Franz Boll, *Sphaera*, Leipzig, 1903.
24. Anton Moortgat, *Die Entstehung der sumerischen Hochkultur*, Leipzig, 1945.
25. Joseph Campbell, *The Hero With a Thousand Faces*, Princeton, USA, 1968.
26. Heinrich Clementz, *Flavius Josephus—Jüdische Altertümer*, Berlin/Vienna, 1923.
27. Theodor Klausner, *Reallexikon für Antike und Christentum*, Stuttgart, 1950.

28. as 5.
29. Karl Simrock, *Die Götterlieder der älteren Edda*, Leipzig, 1947.
30. R.W. Hynek, *Golgatha*, Karlsruhe, 1950.
31. Mary Esther Harding, *Woman's Mysteries*, London, 1935.
32. Max Ebert, *op. cit.*
33. Erich Zehren, *Das Testament der Sterne*, Berlin, 1957.
34. Franz König, *op. cit.*
35. *Ibid.*
36. as 32.
37. Oskar Werner, *Aischylos-Orestie*, Munich, 1949.
38. as 18.
39. Károly Kerény, *The Gods of the Greeks*, London, 1951.
40. J.J. Bachofen, *Der Mythös von Orient und Occident*, ed. M. Schroeter, Munich, 1956.
41. as 33.
42. Will Durant, *Life of Greece, op. cit.*
43. Joachim Spiegel, *Das Werden der ägyptischen Hochkultur*, Heidelberg, 1954.
44. Hartmut Schmökel, *Ur, Assur und Babylon*, Stuttgart, 1955.
45. as 33.
46. Ernst Kocherthaler, *Das Reich der Antike*, Baden-Baden, 1948.
47. as 5.
48. as 7.
49. Adolf Erman, *Die Religion der Ägypter*, Berlin, 1934.
50. Günther Lanczkowski, *Geschichte der Religionen*, Frankfurt, 1972.
51. as 33.
52. Otto Siegfried Reuter, *Germanische Himmelskunde*, Munich, 1934.
53. *Deutsches Revier*, I, 1939.
54. Paul Sträter, S.J., *Katholische Marienkunde*, Paderborn, 1952.

55. as 15.
56. Paul Sträter, S.J., *Maria in der Glaubens-wissenschaft*, Paderborn 1952.
57. C.G. Jung, *Man and His Symbols*, London, 1964.

Chapter 4.
1. Fritz Rienecker, *Das Evangelium des Matthäus*, Wupperthal, 1953.
2. Max von Oppenheim, *Der Tell Halaf und die verschleierte Göttin*, Leipzig, 1908.
3. Julius Schwabe, *op. cit.*
4. Carl Schneider, *op. cit.*
5. C.G. Jung, 'The Relations Between the Ego and the Unconscious' in *Two Essays on Analytical Psychology*, vol.7 of *Collected Works*, London, 1953.
6. Johann Friedrich Kaltwasser, *Plutarchs vergleichende Lebensbeschreibungen*, Leipzig.
7. Karl Friedrich Geldern, *Der Rig-Veda*, Wiesbaden, 1951.
8. Günther Roeder, *Urkunden zur Religion des alten Ägypten*, Jena, 1923.
9. H. Zimmern, *Die Religion der Hethiter*, Leipzig, 1925.
10. Kurt Lange, *Egypt: Architecture, Sculpture, Painting in Three Thousand Years*, London, 1968.
11. Joachim Spiegel, *op. cit.*
12. Hermann Ziock, *Ägypten*, Bonn, 1955.
13. Erich Zehren, *op. cit.*, 1957.
14. Rudolf Otto, Gottheit und Gottheiten der Arier, Berlin, 1957.
15. Homer, *Odyssey*.
16. P.Piper, *Die Nibelungen*, Munich, 1908.
17. G.H.R. von Koenigswald, *The Evolution of Man*, Michigan, USA, 1962.
18. Jacob Burckhardt, *Griechische Kultur*, Berlin, 1950.
19. Martin Persson Nilsson, *History of Greek Religion*, Oxford, 1949.
20. A.E. Jensen, *Das religiöse Weltbild einer frühen*

Kultur, Stuttgart, 1949.

21. Joseph Klausner, *Jesus of Nazareth*, London, 1947.
22. Ernst Kocherthaler, *op. cit.*
23. Franz König, *op. cit.*
24. as 15.
25. Plato, *Republic*.
26. F. Creuzer, *op. cit.*
27. B.C. Olshak, *Tibet, Erde der Götter*, Zurich, 1960.
28. Otto Siegfried Reuter, *op. cit.*
29. Günther Lanczkowski, *op. cit.*
30. Werner Speiser, *Vorderasiatische Kunst*, Berlin, 1952.
31. Pauly-Wissowa, *Real-Enzyklopädie der Klassischen Altertumswissenschaft*, Stuttgart.
32. Apollodorus, *Works*.
33. H. de Terra, *Durch Urwelten am Indus*, Leipzig, 1940.
34. Friedrich Cornelius, *Indogermanische Religionsgeschichte*, Munich, 1942.
35. Hans Bonnet, *Rellexikon der ägyptischen Religionsgeschichte*, Berlin, 1952.
36. J.J. Bachofen, *op. cit.*
37. Erich Zehren, *op. cit.*, 1959.
38. R.H. Codrington, *The Melanesians*, Oxford, 1891.
39. W. Müller, *Die ältesten amerikanischen Sintfluterzählungen*, Bonn, 1930.
40. *Das deutsche Heldenbuch*, Kürschners National-Literatur.
41. as 16.
42. J. Pottinger, *Der Zauberring, Österreichische Volksmärchen*, Vienna, 1957.
43. Siegfried Huber, *Pizarro und seine Brüder*, n.d.
44. W. Eberhard, *Monumenta Seria*, Peking, 1942.
45. E.F. Schmidt, *Persepolis*, Chicago, 1953.
46. Karl F. Kohlenberg, *op. cit.*
47. W. Schadewaldt, *op. cit.*
48. J.J. Tschudi, *Beiträge zur Kenntnis des alten Peru*, 1851.
49. R.B. Dixon, 'Oceanic Mythology', in *Mythology of*

All Races, vol. 9, New York, 1922.

50. Polack, *Manners and Customs of the New Zealanders*, London, 1830.
51. F. Creuzer, *op. cit.*
52. as 35.
53. Albert Schott, *op. cit.*
54. S.N. Kramer, *op. cit.*
55. T. Jacobson, *Frühlicht des Geistes*, Stuttgart, 1954.
56. A. Hohenberger, *Die indische Flutsage und das Matsya-Purana*, Leipzig, 1930.
57. as 46.
58. as 3.
59. as 37.

Chapter 5.
1. W. Krickeberg *et al.*, op. cit.
2. K. Birker-Smith, *Folkwanderings and Culture Drifts in Northern North America*, n.d.
3. Sir G. Grey, *Polynesian Mythology*, London, 1855.
4. J. Gonda, *Die Religionen Indiens*, Stuttgart, 1960.
5. M.N. Durt, *Das Ramayana*, Calcutta, 1894.
6. H. Oldenberg, *Die Weltanschauung der Brahmana-Texte*, Göttingen, 1919.
7. Fritz Kern, *Historia Mundi*, Munich, 1953.
8. R. Pischel, *Leben und Lehre des Buddha*, Leipzig/Berlin, 1926.
9. Iwar Lissner, *Die Kulturen der Menschheit*, Hamburg, 1961.
10. M. Latou, *Les Réligions du Tibet*, Paris, 1957.
11. Helmut Hoffmann, *Religions of Tibet*, London and New York, 1961.
12. L.A. Waddell, *The Buddhism of Tibet or Lamaism*, London, 1934.
13. A. Hohenberger, *op. cit.*
14. H.P.F. Nevermann, *Götter der Südsee*, Stuttgart, 1947.
15. A. Tucci and W. Heissig, *Die Religionen Tibets und der Mongolei*, Stuttgart/Cologne/Mayence, 1970.

16. Ludwig Wolde, *Die Dichtungen und Fragmente des Pindar*, Leipzig, 1942.
17. Hans Baumann, *The Caves of the Great Hunters*, London, 1955.
18. G.R. Steinhäuser, *Das Geheimnis der sterbenden Sterne*, Munich, 1972.
19. Ostrander/Schröder, 'PSI', Berne, 1971.
20. N.A. Rynin, *Interplanetarische Kontakte*, Leningrad, 1932.
21. Johannes Lehmann, *op. cit.*
22. Erich Zehren, *op. cit.*, 1959.
23. Miguel Leon-Portilla and Renate Heuer, *Rückkehr der Götter*, Munich, 1965.
24. Paolo de Gall, *Das Antlitz von Jesus Christus und sein Leichentuch*, Paris, 1972.
25. J.B. Rhine, *Parapsychology*, Oxford, 1958.
26. Kurt Frischler, *op. cit.*
27. Professor Hans Bender, *Parapsychologie*, Darmstadt, 1966.